BY NATALIE MORGAN

HOW TO MAKE

Paper Flowers

AND

Party Decorations

THE COMPLETE BOOK OF PAPER HANDCRAFT

Illustrated by CLARE McCANNA

Grosset & Dunlap, PUBLISHERS
NEW YORK, 1947

D1457980

Table of Contents

Table of Contents

Table of Contents

Table of Contents

Introduction

PAPER has long been a popular material for handcrafts. According to Chinese tradition paper was first developed there about 100 A.D. Long before America was even discovered the custom of providing the dead with paper replicas of the comforts needed for the good life was well established in China.

As a fashionable pastime for women, paper crafts were extremely popular as early as 1660 when Pepys mentioned a paper basket made by his sister, in his famous diary.

When Jane Austen lived and wrote her classics, about 1800, paper crafts were a popular and fashionable recreation with growing girls.

By 1876 such work with paper was so popular that in America books were published about it. "Household Elegancies" is the title of one which illustrated the most elaborate handwork.

By 1905 paper had reached the heights of fashionable popularity as a decorating material at balls.

Today paper crafts are still zooming along. This book includes the most popular of them with easy step-by-step instructions.

It shows you how to make things for your home, for parties, for gifts—pretty things, useful things that are fun to make and cheaper to make than to buy. It gives interesting and inexpensive craft projects for children, projects suited to club and camp activities and for the child at home. It gives crafts of interest to school teachers and to directors of occupational therapy in hospitals and other institutions.

Whether you are new at making pretty paper decorations or whether you would like to try your hand at making different things from paper, you'll find a wealth of information in this book. You'll have fun, too!

Note: In making the various items in this book, you will find Chapter XV on General Directions for Using Crepe Paper most helpful. Each General Direction is designated by a small number which appears to the right of the word in the text. The footnotes appearing at the bottom of the page give the page number on which each particular General Direction appears.

Pink roses and African daisies in a variety of pastel shades are lovely in an old soft blue bowl.

Orange and yellow zinnias take kindly to a bright copper kettle.

To the Dennison Manufacturing Company the author expresses appreciation for permission to show in this book crepe paper flowers and crafts devised in its craft departments and party decorations designed in its Party Bazaars in New York, Chicago and Boston.

CHAPTER I

How to Make Flowers
of Crepe Paper

MAKING ARTIFICIAL FLOWERS is an old and fascinating handcraft. Our great grandmothers made them from scraps of silk and other materials. But it took the development of crepe paper to turn flower making into the art it is today. Now paper flowers are so real looking that we stop to smell them.

Once you've had the thrill of turning bits of paper into pretty flowers, you'll find it intriguing as a hobby. There's a touch of magic in seeing paper blossom into flowers under your own fingers.

Arranging flowers will be more interesting, too, because artificial flowers are easily arranged in various ways. It is fun to copy the arrangements shown in magazines and books, and to express your own personality by creating your own arrangements.

If materials are kept on hand, it is easy to whip up the kind of flowers you want—when you want them—at a low cost. Whether it's jonquils for the breakfast nook or colorful zinnias for a dull spot in the living room, you'll find them easy to make.

Whenever a lot of flowers are needed for a community affair, the annual church or the high school prom, for example, you can turn to this book for instructions and patterns. With its aid you can make them quickly, inexpensively, and have fun in the project.

If you want to make some pin money, flower making is a pleasant and easy way to do it.

Flower making is also wonderful as an occupational therapeutic. Because it is light, simple and cheering, it is an ideal occupation for many invalids and other shut-ins, for use in settlement houses, hospitals and other institutions.

WHAT YOU NEED TO MAKE FLOWERS

FOR as little as forty cents, you can get started on this hobby. Two or three folds of crepe paper, a few wires and a little paste will send you on your way.

Some flowers require several different colors of paper and several different weights of wire. Buying materials for one or two such flowers would be, naturally, rather expensive. But once you have purchased supplies, you'll have enough to make many flowers and many kinds of flowers.

Always keep scraps, no matter how little, of crepe paper for sometimes a flower calls for but a few inches of one color.

Keeping all your materials in a kit is a convenience and an inspiration. A 20-inch box, such as crepe paper comes in, makes an ideal kit.

These are the supplies and equipment for a well rounded kit. *Most of them can be purchased at any chain, stationery, or department store. Flower wires can be bought at those stores that stock materials for flower making.*

Crepe Paper. There are two kinds, single and double. The latter called Duplex, is a convenience in making many flowers, especially those with petals, upper and lower sides, of different colors. However, it's not a necessity as you can always paste two layers of single crepe together to get two tones or a heavier weight.

Stamens and Leaves. For some flowers, commercially made leaves and stamens are more effective than those made of crepe paper. These can be bought at stores carrying supplies for flower making. When they are desirable for a particular flower, "materials required" in this book suggest them.

Scissors. Two pairs are perfect—one pair of heavy sharp shears for cutting through many layers of paper, another lighter weight pair for cutting the petals, etc.

Paste. Ordinary library paste with a stiff stubby brush is best. Glue, mucilage, rubber cement are not suitable.

Paper for Making Patterns. Light weight cardboard, heavy wrapping paper or note paper is necessary for this operation. The folder in which crepe paper is packed is perfect.

Tissue or Tracing Paper. Only a small amount is needed to trace patterns.

Pins . . . Pencil . . . Ruler

Wire Cutters or Pliers. This tool is useful, though not necessary except in those cases where an extra heavy stem wire, a No. 7 or No. 15, is required.

Wires. The chart which appears on page 241 should be helpful for reference. Directions for making the flowers given in this book specify types of wires needed.

LOOK BEFORE YOU LEAP

IF YOU want to, you can turn to the directions for making the first flower offered in this book and fall to. However, we do not recommend it. Your progress will be faster, your results more successful if you first practice some of the steps required in making all flowers. Therefore, we urge that you get a little crepe paper, a few pieces of flower wire and some paste and try the tricks listed in Chapter XV where General Directions for making flowers from crepe paper are given.

In the step-by-step directions for making the various flowers which follow, reference is frequently made to these instructions. It's an excellent idea not only to practice the processes numbered 1 to 7, but also to read all of the General Directions from 1 through 14. If you familiarize yourself with them now you may not have to turn to the pages of General Directions every time they're referred to. However, if in doubt, take no chance. Read the directions indicated by the small numbers appearing from time to time.* **Failure to cut a "strip of crepe paper" properly, for example, may make your flower a dismal flop.**

> * *All of the small numbers which appear to the right of a word in the text are referred to in the footnotes at the bottom of each page. These footnotes give the page on which the particular number referred to appears.*
>
> *For example:* "Make Patterns" [12] *refers to instruction No. 12 on how to make patterns for paper flowers. This number 12 is referred to in the footnote which tells you that 12 appears in the General Directions on page 229.*
>
> *Another example is* "Cup." [4] *This 4 refers to the directions for cupping paper flowers. It is referred to in the footnote on the bottom of the page which tells you that General Direction 4 appears on page 224.*

Jonquils never let you down. They're easy to make,
easy to arrange.

Fig. 1 Jonquil.

THIS DELICATE SPRING flower is the perfect masquerader. See one in a vase and you must look twice. Is it a jonquil in "the flesh" or just crepe paper acting the part? Probably it's because the jonquil's so highly stylized petals that it lends itself so well to the crepe paper copyist.

At any rate, it's a lovely flower and a perfect one for your initiation into flower making.

If you want to make some for a flower pot, three are enough. You can pack the pot with waste paper to hold the stems erect and then cover the top with pebbles or with shredded brown crepe paper. Jonquils, of course, are lovely in a mixed bouquet. Try them with several tulips of various colors, say lavender, purple and deep pink.

Materials Needed to Make One Dozen:
   1 fold crepe paper yellow for petals
   1 fold crepe paper dark yellow for trumpet
   1 fold crepe paper leafy green for leaves and stem
   1 fold crepe paper light brown or sand for sheath
   1 spool wire No. 1 or 2
   1 dozen wires No. 9 or 10
   Paste, cardboard, tissue paper

[4]

NOTE: *Duplex crepe in two shades of green can be used for the leaves in place of the leaf green specified.*

Step 1. Make the Patterns.[12] The outlines for petals, leaves, trumpet and sheath are shown in Figures 8, 9, 10 and 11.

Step 2. Make the Pistil (*Fig. 2*). In the jonquil this part of the flower, which is always in the center, is a toothpick size affair, about 1½-inches long. To make it, cut a strip of the darker yellow crepe across

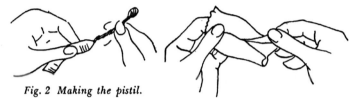

Fig. 2 *Making the pistil.*

Fig. 3 *Making the trumpet.*

Fig. 4 *The sheath.*

Fig. 5 *Putting the blossom together.*

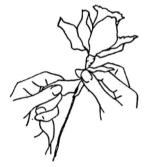

Fig. 6 *Wrapping the stem with green crepe.*

the grain ½-inch wide and 2-inches long. Stretch it, and then roll it tightly and at a diagonal until you have a tight twisted roll a little fatter at one end than the other. To do this is easy. Here's how: Hold the strip in your left hand between your thumb and forefinger. With the thumb and forefinger of your other hand crush the right end, forming a little wad of paper at the end. Beginning with

See General Direction 1, *p.* 223; 12, *p.* 229

the ball, roll the paper between the thumb and forefinger of the right hand diagonally downward, around and around to the end.

Step 3. Place the Patterns in Position.[13] Cut for each flower one trumpet of darker yellow, six petals of lighter yellow, two or four leaves, one sheath of sand. If you're using Duplex for the leaves, cut only one or two.

Fig. 7 Adding the leaves.   *Fig. 8 Jonquil petal pattern, actual size.*

Step 4. Shape the Parts. (*a*) *Trumpet.* Flute [3] each one of the six scallops once and cup [4] the trumpet through the center. Paste the opposite straight edges together overlapping the sides about 1/4-inch at the bottom and tapering off to practically nothing at the top (*Fig. 3*). (*b*) *Petals.* With the rougher side of the crepe up, cup each petal slightly, just enough to give a turned back effect. (*c*) *Paste two leaves together.*[10] Omit this step if using Duplex. Keep rougher side of crepe, which is the "right" side, out. Vein the leaf in this way: put it on a flat surface and draw a line with your fingernail or the point of a knitting needle down the center from tip to base. (*d*) *Sheath (Fig. 4).* This should look like a withered leaf. To get that appearance, wad the sheath up tightly in your hand, and then pull it back gently into shape.

See General Direction 13, *p.* 229; 3, *p.* 224; 4, *p.* 224; 10, *p.* 228

[6]

Step 5. Put the Blossom Together (*Fig. 5*). Place the pistil inside the trumpet with the end of the pistil even with the bottom of the

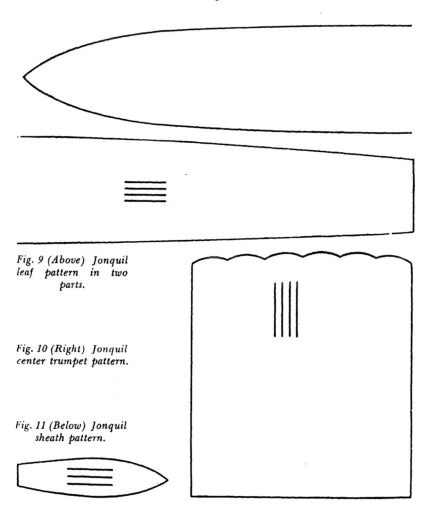

Fig. 9 (Above) Jonquil leaf pattern in two parts.

Fig. 10 (Right) Jonquil center trumpet pattern.

Fig. 11 (Below) Jonquil sheath pattern.

trumpet. Apply paste to the bottom (inside) of the trumpet and press it against the pistil. Paste three petals evenly spaced, around the trumpet, with the top edges just below the fluting. Paste the other three petals in a second row placing them between the petals of the first. Tie with a 10-inch length of spool wire.[6]

See **General Direction** 6, *p.* 226

[7]

Step 6. Add the Stem and Leaves (*Fig. 6 and 7*). To make the jonquil stems thick enough, wrap them three separate times, using a strip of green crepe paper 1-inch wide and 20-inches long. On the first wrapping, 1-inch below the base of the flower, add two No. 10 wires 14-inches long. Wrap the stem a second time. On the third wrapping 1-inch below the flower, wrap in the sheath and 3-inches from the bottom of the stem wrap in the leaves on opposite sides of the stem.

Curl the leaves back slightly at the top [5] and the flower is complete.

Tulips

Fig. 12 Tulip.

THEIR BRILLIANT COLORS and simple graceful forms make the tulip a delight to copy in crepe paper. Your first effort may not be a perfect one, but it's certain to reward you by looking like a tulip and by being bright.

There are, of course, all sorts of tulips. Some are slender and pointed like a candle's flame, others are round and plump in a hearty, healthy way; some have color tinged edges, and one, at least—the parrot tulip—has feathery curled petals.

The patterns given here are for a favorite garden variety. After

See **General Direction** 5, *p.* 225

you've made a few, you will want to branch out with additional colors, tinting, and perhaps shapes. You can whittle down the sides, point the tops, and, guided by a flower catalog make a handsome assortment of these history-and-tradition rich flowers.

Materials Needed to Make One Dozen:

1 fold crepe paper yellow, red or any tulip shade for petals
1 fold crepe paper light green for leaves, and stem
1 fold crepe paper leafy green for leaves
1 fold crepe paper black for pistil
1 fold crepe paper light yellow green for the center
1 spool wire No. 1 or 2
1 dozen wires No. 9 or 10
Paste, cardboard, tissue paper

NOTE: *Tulips can be made by using Duplex crepe. Patterns and directions are the same for both single and Duplex, or double, crepe.*

Step 1. Make the Patterns.[12] The outlines for the petals and leaves are shown in Figures 16 and 17.

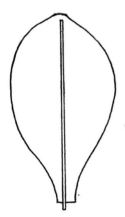

Fig. 13 (Left) Vein in the petal.

Fig. 14 (Right) The center of the tulip.

Step 2. Cut the Petals, Leaves and Center.[13] Cut six petals and four leaves (or two if using Duplex Crepe) for each flower. For the center, cut from light yellow green crepe a strip 3½-inches long and 3-inches wide.[1]

Step 3. Prepare the Petals, Leaves, Center and Stamens. Place petal, smoother side of crepe paper up, on table. Paste a 3½-inch piece of spool wire, wrapped [7] in the same color as the petals, down the center of the flower to form a vein.[11] For wrapping use a strip ¼-inch

---

See General Direction 12, *p.* 229; 13, *p.* 229; 1, *p.* 223; 7, *p.* 227; 11, *p.* 229

wide. This will leave ½-inch extending like a little handle (*Fig. 13*). Vein each petal in that way with spool wire. Cup[4] each one slightly in the center. Leaves are made of two thicknesses of crepe so paste two leaves together[10] if you're using single crepe. To give the leaves a veined effect, draw a line down the center of each, from base to tip, with your fingernail or the point of a knitting needle.

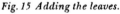

Fig. 15 *Adding the leaves.*

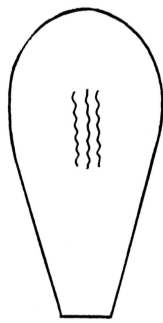

Fig. 16 *Tulip petal pattern.*

Curl the tips of the leaves backwards slightly.[5] For the Center (*Fig. 14*) fold the 3½-inch strip of light yellow green paper down the center across the grain. (Don't crease the doubled edge.) Roll this with the doubled edge up and secure the end with paste. Make five stamens by wrapping spool wire cut to 2-inch lengths, with black crepe cut ¼-inch wide.[7] To make the stamens thick enough, wrap each one three times. Place the stamens around the light yellow green roll and, using spool wire, tie them in position with their ends extending above the top of the roll.[6]

Step 4. Put the Flower Together. Paste three petals around the center, applying the paste lightly at the base of the petals. Paste the other

See General Direction 4, *p.* 224; 10, *p.* 228; 5, *p.* 225; 7, *p.* 227; 6, *p.* 226

three in a second row, placing them exactly between the first three. Tie them at the base with a 10-inch length of spool wire.

Step 5. Add the Stem and Leaves.[7,8,9] At the base, start wrapping the stem with a 1-inch strip of lighter green crepe. About 1-inch below the flower add two 14-inch lengths of No. 9 or No. 10 wire and com-

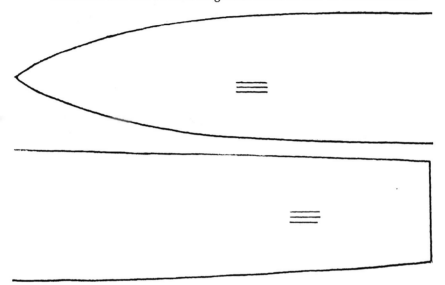

Fig. 17 Tulip leaf pattern in two parts.

plete wrapping. Wrap a second time for additional thickness, this time inserting the two leaves, on opposite sides, about 3-inches from the bottom of the stem (*Fig. 15*).

Step 6. Final Shaping. With your fingers inside the outer row of flowers, shape them by curving the veining wires out and up. Then shape the inner row, and, if necessary, curl back the leaves a bit more.[5] A natural look can be given by twisting the end of one leaf a bit. The tulip is now complete.

Another popular way to make the tulip is to vein the leaves. If you prefer the heavy veined look and also the stiffer leaf that comes with veining, cut a length of spool wire or No. 9 or 10 wire a bit longer than the leaf. Wrap[7] it with a 1/4-inch wide strip[1] of green crepe paper pasting it carefully at the top and bottom of the wire. Paste the wire down the center length of the leaf.[11] Bouquets of waxed tulips are also popular. Fortunately the flower is an easy one to wax. See Page 45.

See General Direction 7, *p.* 227; 8, *p.* 227; 9, *p.* 227; 5, *p.* 225; 1, *p.* 223; 11, *p.* 229

Fig. 18 Gardenia.

THIS FLOWER OF many uses makes up beautifully and, surprisingly easily in crepe paper. A few are always decorative in a low bowl; with a bud, one or two make the most popular of all corsages; and finally, as a party favor, the gardenia is widely used.

Materials Needed to Make One Dozen:
 1 fold crepe paper white for petals
 1 fold crepe paper leaf green for stems and leaves
 1 spool wire No. 1
 Paste, cardboard, tissue paper; artificial rose leaves (optional)

NOTE: *White Duplex (or double) crepe is perfect for gardenias as each petal must be made of two thicknesses of crepe. If you can get Duplex crepe follow the directions below, but make petals of one thickness, not two. As glistening green leaves add so much to the appearance of the gardenia, it is recommended that ready-made rose leaves be used. If you can't get them, use the leaf pattern given; paste two layers of crepe together to make each leaf double [10] and wire each leaf with a 3-inch length of No. 9 wire.[11]*

Step 1. Make the Patterns.[12] The outlines for the petal and leaf are shown in Figures 21 and 22.

Step 2. Cut the Petals and Leaves.[13] Cut fourteen petals from Duplex crepe or twenty-eight from single crepe, pasting the petals together in pairs.[10] Cut one leaf for each flower and one for each bud from Duplex crepe, or two from single crepe, pasting the two together. If using a ready-made rose leaf, trim its edges to the shape of the gardenia leaf pattern.

***

See General Direction 10, *p.* 228; 11, *p.* 229; 12, *p.* 229; 13, *p.* 229

Step 3. Prepare the Petals and Leaves. Flute [8] three petals once in the center; curl two at the top sides over a scissors blade.[5] Roll six petals backwards and leave the remaining three plain. Cup all the petals in this way: Cup the fluted and plain ones deeply in the center; cup

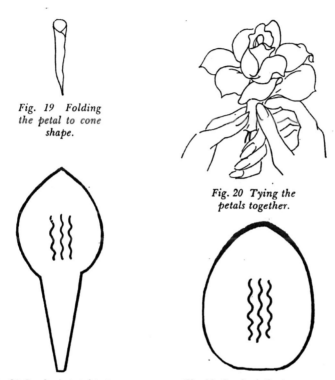

Fig. 19 *Folding the petal to cone shape.*

Fig. 20 *Tying the petals together.*

Fig. 21 *Gardenia petal pattern.*

Fig. 22 *Gardenia leaf pattern.*

the others below the center and less deeply. Wire [11] each leaf through the center, with a 3-inch length of spool wire. This step is naturally omitted if you're using ready-made leaves.

Step 4. Put the Petals Together. Hold each petal in the position described below with a little paste. The petals of the gardenia should be laid in position smoothly, not gathered at the base. Begin with a plain petal and fold it to a cone shape (*Fig. 19*). Place a second plain petal opposite the first one, and paste it smoothly in place, keeping the top edges even. Opposite it, add a fluted petal, then

---

See General Direction 3, *p.* 224; 5, *p.* 225; 11, *p.* 229

(opposite, again) a plain one, then two fluted ones. With all the top edges even, this group of six petals forms the compact center of the flower. Add the other petals with the cupping backward so that they fall away from the center. Add the two with the curled edges last of all (*Fig. 20*).

Tie the petals together with a 10-inch length of spool wire.[6]

Step 5. Add the Stem and Leaves.[7,8,9] With a ½-inch wide strip of green crepe wrap the stem once. Wrap it a second time, inserting a leaf close to the flower. When this is done, you are ready to stand back and admire your handiwork.

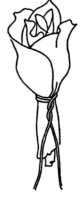

Fig. 23 Gardenia Bud.

A CORSAGE OF TWO gardenias is improved by the addition of a bud. Make it just like the center of the flower, using three petals only. Tie it with spool wire (*Fig. 23*), wrap it with the green crepe and insert a green leaf close to the bud. Add the bud to the flower stem on the second wrapping so that its top comes about 1-inch above the top of the flower itself.

Although the natural color of the gardenia is white, it is often made in pastel and bright colors for corsages, for party favors and for dressing table novelties. As a trick for giving an inexpensive gift individuality, the gardenia is widely used. For example, an inexpensive box of dusting powder can be elevated to the gift class by having a pale pink, let us say, gardenia tied to its top. Such tying is generally done with spool wire. Punch two tiny holes in the box top. Thread a piece of spool wire through them and hold the gardenia in place by twisting the spool wire ends around its stem.

See General Direction 6, *p.* 226; 7, *p.* 227; 8, *p.* 227; 9, *p.* 227

Fig. 24 Rose.

WHY IS THE ROSE the most popular flower to make? Perhaps because, looking so complicated, it's amazing to see the paper come to life and bloom under your fingers. Once you have made one rose, you can make other varieties because a rose is a rose—and they're all—little, big, full-blown, tightly curled, red, yellow, pink, white—basically alike.

Materials Needed to Make One Dozen:

    1 fold crepe paper pink for petals
    1 fold crepe paper white for petals
    1 fold crepe paper leaf green for leaves, and calyx
    1 fold crepe paper moss green for leaves, calyx, and stems
    1 spool wire No. 1 or 2
    6 wires No. 7
    1 dozen wires No. 9 or 10
    3 dozen rose leaves (optional)
    Paste, cardboard, tissue paper, wire pliers or cutters

NOTE: *Any two shades of green suitable for leaves and stems can be used. If necessary, one color will do the trick, but not so effectively. Duplex crepe pink white, and single crepe pink can be used for the petals and Duplex in two shades of green for the leaves.*

Step 1. Make the Patterns.[12] The outlines for the petals, calyxes, and leaves are shown in Figures 31, 32, 33, and 34.

Step 2. Cut the Petals, Calyxes and Leaves.[13] From pink crepe paper cut eleven petals and put them to one side. Cut five more pink, five white and paste [10] them together.

    Cut one calyx from green Duplex crepe or two from single crepe

See General Direction 12, *p.* 229; 13, *p.* 229; 10, *p.* 228

pasting [10] the two together. Roll each point slightly between your thumb and forefinger to take away the stiff look. Cut three leaves for each leaf spray, one smaller leaf and two larger ones. Make from one to four sprays for each flower, as described under step 5. If you

Fig. 25 Fluting.

Fig. 26 Cupping.

do not have Duplex crepe, cut the leaves from the two shades of leaf green and paste the two shades together.

Step 3. Shape the Petals. Shape them in the following groups and keep each group separate.

Group 1. Flute (*Fig. 25*) [3] five pink petals once in the center top. Cup (*Fig. 26*) [4] these five rather deeply in the very center.

Fig. 27 Curling over a knitting needle.

Fig. 28 Curling over a scissors blade.

Fig. 29 Making the center of a rose.

Group 2. Curl (*Fig. 27*) [5] six pink petals over a knitting needle. Cup these only slightly. Cup them below center.

Group 3. These are the five double (pink white) petals. With the white side up, curl (*Fig. 28*) the tops over a scissors blade. Cup [4] them slightly near the lower part.

Step 4. Put the Flower Together. Hold each petal in the position described with a bit of paste. Take one petal from Group One and roll it into a tight bud (*Fig. 29*). Place a second petal, from the same group around it, overlapping the first about half way. Arrange the remaining three from Group One in the same way, but do not wrap them around so tightly. Now arrange Group Two petals. Place these so that their tops are slightly higher than Group One. Otherwise arrange them as you did in Group One.

See General Direction 10, *p.* 228; 3, *p.* 224; 4, *p.* 224; 5, *p.* 225

Arrange Group Three still higher. Their tops should extend about ¼-inch above those of Group Two and each petal should overlap the previous by about one-half. As the rose has now begun to bloom, you will see where to add the petals and how much to over-

Fig. 30 Wrapping the stem.

lap them. Also, you will let these petals fall away from the center to give the rose a more opened look.

Tie [6] the petals together 1-inch from the base with two pieces of spool wire about 8-inches long. Cover the base of the flower with paste and put the calyx, with the darker side out, around it.

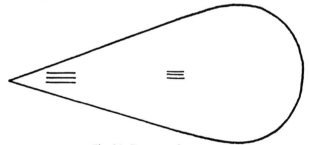

Fig. 31 Rose petal pattern.

Step 5. Add the Stem and Leaves [7,8,9] (*Fig. 30*). At the calyx start wrapping the stem with a strip of crepe paper cut 1-inch wide and doubled lengthwise through the middle. About 2-inches below the calyx, add a 15-inch length of No. 7 wire. Finish wrapping the stem. Wrap a second time, this time inserting one to four sprays of leaves. As you make up a bouquet, insert the leaf sprays at different intervals on the twelve stems. Avoid the cluttered look that results when the sprays emerge from the stems at exactly the same spot.

See General Direction 6, *p.* 226; 7, *p.* 227; 8, *p.* 227; 9, *p.* 227

[17]

Leaf Sprays of Crepe Paper. If you have cut your leaves from crepe paper, make them up into sprays in this way: To the back or lighter side of one smaller leaf, paste [11] down the center length, a 4½-inch length of No. 9 or 10 wire. To the backs of two larger leaves, paste 3-inch lengths of wire in the same way. Wrap the ½-inch extending from one leaf, with a very

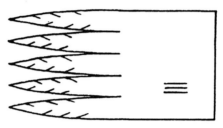

Fig. 32 Rose calyx pattern.

Fig. 33 Rose leaf pattern.

Fig. 34 Rose leaf pattern.

narrow (¼-inch wide) strip of green crepe paper. One inch below the leaf, insert on opposite sides of the stem the other two leaves and continue wrapping to the end.

Bend some of the flowers a bit, and tip the leaf sprays back from the stem. In arranging a bouquet, vary this a little with each flower so that the bouquet will not have a machine-made look.

See General Direction 11, *p.* 229

Fig. 35 Dogwood.

Dogwood

ALTHOUGH CREPE PAPER dogwood is popular for home use, it enjoys its greatest popularity in mass decorations—for spring dances, pageants—for display use in windows, club rooms and hotel lobbies.

When great masses are to be made and speed is important, natural branches are often used. Crepe blossoms and leaves are wrapped to the real branches with just enough crepe paper to hold them in place. When real branches aren't used, and a close-to-nature effect is highly desirable, real twigs are wrapped to the ends of the wire ones.

Materials Needed to Make Three Sprays:
1 fold crepe paper white for petals
1 fold crepe paper light yellow for centers
1 fold crepe paper leafy green for centers
1 fold crepe paper brown for stems
3 spools wire No. 1 or 2
9 wires No. 7
3 wires No. 15
Paste, cardboard, tissue paper, pliers or wire cutters

NOTE: *Duplex crepe in two shades of green is excellent for the leaves if the sprays are to bear close inspection. For hall decorations single crepe is entirely satisfactory.*

Step 1. Make the Patterns.[12] The outlines for dogwood patterns are shown in Figures 40, 41 and 42. Note that there are two petals of one size, two of another in each dogwood blossom.

Step 2. Cut the Petals, Leaves and Center.[13] From white crepe paper cut two petals of each size for each blossom. Cut enough for about ten

See General Direction 12, *p*. 229: 13, *p*. 229

[19]

blossoms for each spray. Cut twelve leaves for each spray. Two leaves are added below each blossom, and two more toward the end of the spray. For the centers, cut from the following colors for each flower a strip[1] 1-inch wide across the grain, 2-inches long: dark brown, leaf green, light yellow.

Fig. 36 Petal and center.

Fig. 37 Petals fastened to the center.

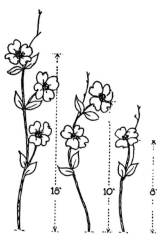

Fig. 38 Stems and leaves added.

Fig. 39 The main stem.

Step 3. Prepare the Petals and Centers (*Fig. 36*). For the centers place the three, brown, green, and yellow strips directly over each other. Stretch them, and along one long edge cut them into fine fringe ½-inch deep.[2] With the three still together like a triple deck sandwich, roll them together tightly and paste the end down.

Tint the center top of each petal with brown crepe paper moistened with water. Cup[4] each petal slightly through the center.

See General Direction 1, *p.* 223; 2, *p.* 223; 4, *p.* 224

Step 4. Put the Flower Together (*Fig. 37*). Paste petals around center, two smaller ones opposite two larger ones. Tie [6] with a 10-inch length of spool wire.

Step 5. Add the Stem and Leaves (*Fig. 38*).[1,7,8,9] Cut a strip of leaf green crepe ½-inch wide and 12-inches long. Start wrapping the stem at the base of the flower. Two and one-half inches from the base, add two leaves, one on each side of the stem. Cut three No. 7

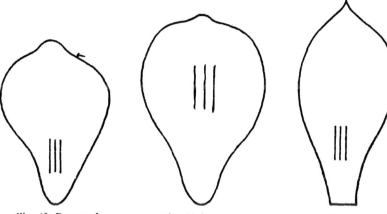

Fig. 40 Dogwood   Fig. 41 Dogwood   Fig. 42 Dogwood
petal pattern.   petal pattern.   leaf pattern.

wires into 18-inch, 10-inch and 8-inch lengths. Wrap each with strips of brown crepe cut ¾-inch wide across the grain. If possible wrap a real twig in at each end. To the longest of the three wires, add three blossoms each with two leaves about 2-inches below the blossom: to the 10-inch wire, add two blossoms with their accompanying leaves, and to the shortest wire add one blossom with its two leaves.

To make the Main Stem (*Fig. 39*) take a 24-inch length of No. 15 wire and wrap it twice with dark brown crepe cut ¾-inch wide across the grain. If possible, wrap a real twig in at the top. Toward the top, wrap in two blossoms, and below them two leaves. As the wrapping proceeds, insert the 18-inch, 10-inch, and 8-inch branches. Near its center reinforce the stem by adding a 12-inch length of No. 15 wire.

Bend the stems, and shape the flowers and leaves as your eye dictates.

When this is done the dogwood is ready to say, "Look! Spring is here!"

See General Direction 6, *p.* 226; 1, *p.* 223; 7, *p.* 227; 8, *p.* 227; 9, *p.* 227

California

Poppies

Fig. 43 California poppy.

ALL THAT THE name signifies, these are the sunniest and gayest of flowers. In a deep blue, copper or brass bowl they are particularly lovely.

Materials Needed to Make One Dozen:

 1 fold crepe paper yellow, red or orange for petals and centers
 1 fold crepe paper leafy green for leaves and stems
 1 spool wire No. 1 or 2
 1 dozen wires No. 9 or 10
 Black India Ink to tint centers
 Paste, cardboard, tissue paper

NOTE: *The most beautiful effect can be secured easily by using Duplex crepe for petals and leaves. For the petals, a crepe that is an orange yellow on one side, and a canary yellow on the opposite is perfect. The canary forms the outside of the petals. For the leaves, two shades of green, one very light, the other dark, are ideal, but one will do. If you can't get Duplex, you can make your own by cutting each leaf and petal double and pasting [10] them together. Use single crepe for wrapping stems.*

Step 1. Make the Patterns.[12] The outlines for petals and leaves are shown in Figures 46 and 47.

Step 2. Cut the Petals, Leaves and Centers.[13] For each flower cut four petals and five leaves. If you use regular, or single thickness crepe paper, cut eight petals, ten leaves, and paste [10] two of each together. For the center of each flower, cut from the same crepe used for the petals, a strip [1] 1½-inches wide and 3-inches long. Stretch it and then slash its entire length on one side into fringe [2] cutting at about

---

See General Direction 10, *p.* 228; 12, *p.* 229; 13, *p.* 229; 1, *p.* 223; 2, *p.* 223

⅛-inch intervals and making each cut about 1-inch deep. This fringe forms the stamens. Tip their points with black, using black India Ink, or a little pencil-like roll of black crepe paper moistened at the end in water. When dry, gather the plain edge with your fingers and tie [6] with a 4-inch length of spool wire (*Fig. 44*).

Fig. 44 (Left) Stamens tied.

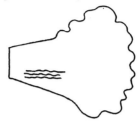

Fig. 45 (Right) Fluted petal.

Step 3. Shape the Flower. Flute [3] the top of each petal slightly, and along the entire edge (*Fig. 45*). Cup [4] each petal just below center.

Step 4. Put the Flower Together. Paste the four petals lightly around the base of the stamens, letting them overlap about half, then tie [6] them together with an 18-inch length of No. 10 wire.

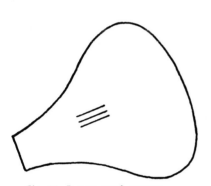

Fig. 46 Poppy petal pattern.   Fig. 47 Poppy leaf pattern.

Step 5. Make the Leaf Branches.[7,8,9] Make two leaf branches for each flower using a 7-inch length of No. 10 wire for each. On one wire, wrap in two leaves, on the other, three. With each, place one leaf at the tip, and the others about 2-inches apart on opposite sides of the stems. Wrap the stems with a ½-inch strip of green crepe paper.

Step 6. Put the Flower and Leaf Branches Together. Using a ½-wide strip of green, wrap the flower stem, inserting one leaf branch 3-inches below the flower, the other 6-inches below, and on opposite sides of the stem.

See General Direction 6, *p.* 226; 3, *p.* 224; 4, *p.* 224; 7, *p.* 227; 8, *p.* 227; 9, *p.* 227

Fig. 48 African Daisy.

African Daisy

THIS GRACEFUL FLOWER is a boon to home decorations for there's no limit to the colors it can be made in. White, pink, pale yellow and American Beauty Red, are the colors usually seen, but it can be made in fall shades—yellow, orange, and red. A medley of purple, lavender, pinks, and reds can be beautiful. The directions are for a two-tone flower, pink and white.

Materials Needed to Make One Dozen:

   1 fold crepe paper white for petals
   1 fold crepe paper pink for petals
   1 fold crepe paper yellow for centers
   1 fold crepe paper light green for centers and leaves
   1 spool wire No. 1 or 2
   4 wires No. 9 or 10
   Paste, cardboard, tissue paper

NOTE: *For perfection, the petals should be made double thickness. Duplex crepe therefore, is perfect to use.*

Step 1. Make the Patterns.[12] The outlines for the petals and leaves are shown in Figures 51 and 52.

Step 2. Cut the Petals, Leaves and Center. These petals are so fine, it is easier to cut them free hand, simply using the pattern as a guide. Cut a strip [10] of petals and slash [10] it into long pointed shapes. Open the strip up and cut it into 5-inch lengths.

   For the leaves, cut a strip [1] of light green, 4-inches wide, and proceed as with the petals. Cut the leaf strip apart with five points to

See General Direction 12, *p.* 229; 10, *p.* 228; 1, *p.* 223

[24]

each section. For the center (*Fig. 49*) cut three identical strips 1-inch wide and 4-inches long of light green, light yellow, and the color used for the flower. Along one edge slash these strips into a fine fringe ½-inch deep.[2] Roll the green into a tight little cylinder, and paste down the end. Place the other two strips together, one on top of the other, and roll the two slightly around the green, with their tops slightly higher than the green. Hold the end down with paste.

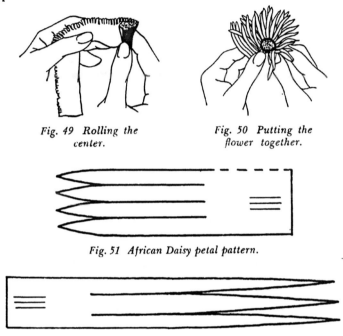

Fig. 49 *Rolling the center.*   Fig. 50 *Putting the flower together.*

Fig. 51 *African Daisy petal pattern.*

Fig. 52 *African Daisy foliage pattern.*

Step 3. Shape the Petals and Leaves. Curl [5] the ends of both slightly over a scissors blade.

Step 4. Put the Flower Together (*Fig. 50*). Place the petal strip around the center, gathering it in at the base so that it encircles the center once. Tie [6] the strip to the base with a 10-inch length of spool wire.

Step 5. Add the Stem and Leaves.[7,8,9] Wrap the stem with a ½-inch strip of light green. Just below the base of the flower, add two No. 10 wires about 12-inches long. Add the leaves at pleasing intervals along the stem. One group should be fairly near the flower.

See General Direction 2, *p.* 223; 5, *p.* 225; 6, *p.* 226; 7, *p.* 227; 8, *p.* 227; 9, *p.* 227

Fig. 53 Zinnia.

Zinnias

THESE DIRECTIONS are for a simplified variety. The petals are cut from one color and in one long strip which is arranged around a fringed center. If you prefer more subtle coloring, use these directions, but elaborate on the coloring. The simplest way to do that is to make the petals of a double thickness of crepe paper, one side red, the other orange for example. You can paste the petals cut from single crepe together [10] or you can use Duplex crepe. Another way to elaborate upon the coloring is to use a number of blending shades of paper for one flower. The blending can be carried out further by tinting [14] the tips of the petals slightly with dry colors. In short, the zinnia can be a simple or complex affair.

Materials Needed to Make One Dozen:
>1 fold crepe paper red or orange for petals
>1 fold crepe paper leafy green for calyx, leaves and stem
>1 spool wire No. 1 or 2
>6 wires No. 7
>Paste, cardboard, tissue paper

NOTE: *Duplex crepe in two tones of green may be used for the leaves and calyx.*

Step 1. Make the Patterns. [12] The outlines for petals, leaves and calyx are shown in Figures 56, 57 and 58.

Step 2. Cut the Petals, Leaves, Center and Calyx. [13] Cut a strip [1] of the crepe paper selected for the petals 2½-inches wide and 25-inches long. Fold it in half with the grain, and refold it to eight thicknesses. Place pattern in position and cut the petal strip. This 25-inch strip forms one flower.

See General Direction 10, *p.* 228; 14, *p.* 231; 12, *p.* 229; 13, *p.* 229; 1, *p.* 223

Cut one calyx for each flower. Cut four to six leaves for each flower. With your fingernail or the point of a knitting needle, draw in the veins as indicated by the dotted lines in the pattern. For the center, from the crepe paper used for the petals, cut across the grain a strip 1¾-inches wide and 6-inches long. Stretch this strip and fold it through the center with the grain. Along one edge slash the crepe into a very fine fringe, ½-inch deep.[2]

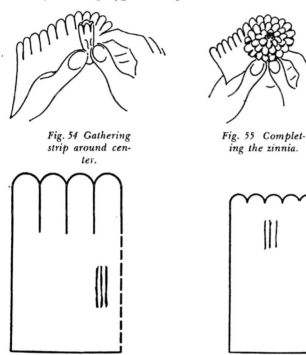

Fig. 54 Gathering strip around center.

Fig. 55 Completing the zinnia.

Fig. 56 Zinnia petal leaf pattern.

Fig. 57 Zinnia calyx pattern.

Step 3. Shape the Petals and Center. Curl[5] the petals back slightly over a scissors blade. The rougher side is the top side of the petals. Roll the fringed center strip tightly and paste down the loose end.

Step 4. Put the Flower Together (*Fig. 54*). Commencing at either end of the petal strip, gather it around the center. The first row of petals should be ¼-inch above the center. Continue gathering the strip around the center in such a way that each row of petals is about ¼-inch higher than the previous one. Full the first three or four

See General Direction 2, *p.* 223; 5, *p.* 225

[27]

rows in rather generously, gradually reducing the amount of fullness as you encircle the center again and again (*Fig. 55*). On the
last row there should be practically no fullness. Tie [6] the base with
a 10-inch length of spool wire. Brush the calyx lightly with paste
and press it against the base of the flower. About ⅛-inch of the
scalloped edge of the calyx should lie against the underside of the
last row of petals. Under the base of the flower, pinch the calyx
together.

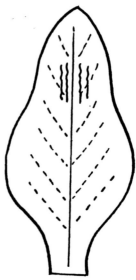

*Fig. 58 Zinnia leaf pat-
tern. When cutting the
pattern, be sure that
the grain of the crepe
runs the long way as in-
dicated by the three
small lines on the pat-
tern.*

Step 5. Add the Stem and Leaves.[7,8,9] Cut a strip of green crepe across
the grain, ¾-inch wide, and at the base of the calyx start wrapping
the stem inserting at once a No. 7 wire 12-inches long. Half way
down the stem reinforce it with another No. 7 wire, this one 6-
inches long. Wrap to the end. Start wrapping the stem a second
time, inserting the leaves on opposite sides of the stem. Insert the
first pair about 2-inches from the base of the flower. Add the other
leaves about 3-inches apart.

Step 6. Shape the Flower. Push the petals away from the center and
downward to give a flat effect. Fluff out the fringed center a bit to
take away any stiff look. Cup [4] the leaves very lightly toward the
stem and curve the upper part of the stem slightly. The completed
zinnia will reward you for your effort.

See General Direction 6, *p.* 226; 7, *p.* 227; 8, *p.* 227; 9, *p.* 227; 4, *p.* 224

Fig. 59 Carnation.

Carnations

FOR PARTY FAVORS, gift wrapped packages, especially on Mother's Day, window displays, hair-do's and similar purposes the carnation is in a class by itself. Giant size flowers, as big as pumpkins, are often used for window displays and platform decorations for Mother's Day programs. It is easy to make, and the variety of colors offered in crepe paper are an inspiration.

Materials Needed to Make One Dozen:
> 1 fold crepe paper white, red or pink for the flower
> 1 fold crepe paper leafy green for stems, leaves, and calyx
> 1 spool wire No. 1 or 2
> 1 dozen wires No. 9 or 10
> Paste, cardboard, tissue paper

Step 1. Make the Patterns.[12] The outlines of petals, calyx and leaves are shown in Figures 64, 65 and 66.

Step 2. Cut the Petals, Leaves, Calyx. Cut a strip of the crepe paper selected for the blossoms, 3-inches wide and 30-inches long. Stretch it until it measures 34½-inches. Fold it and refold it, then cut a

See General Direction 12, *p.* 229

strip of petals [13] cutting down on the sides only as far as the dotted lines (*Fig. 64*). For each flower, cut six leaves and one calyx.[13]

Step 3. Shape the Petals and Leaves. Open up the petal strip. With your fingers, press each petal into about three pleats. These are the kind of pleats a child makes when folding a paper fan. Flute [3] the top of each petal once. If you find it easier, you may press in the pleats with a scissors blade (*Fig. 61*).

Fig. 60 *Cutting a strip of petals.*

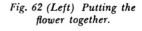

Fig. 61 *(Above)* Shaping petals.

Fig. 62 *(Left)* Putting the flower together.

Step 4. Put the Flower Together. With your fingers, gather the petal strip into carnation shape. Easy to do! Here's a hint on procedure: Hold the end of the strip at its base in your left hand. Gather the strip with the right hand working the paper into the left (*Fig. 62*). As you do this, turn the crepe in the left hand slowly around. When the strip is completely gathered, tie [6] it 1-inch from the base with a 10-inch length of spool wire. Cut off the surplus crepe beneath the twisted wires, at an angle from each side, so that a pointed base remains. Tie the base with another piece of spool wire, right over the first, but bring the ends down on opposite sides and twist them together directly under the flower.

Paste the calyx around the base, leaving the points well up and loose, on the back of the carnation.

See General Direction 13. *p.* 229; 3, *p.* 224; 5, *p.* 225; 6. *p.* 226

Step 5. Add Stem and Leaves (*Fig. 63*).[7,8,9] For wrapping the stem cut a strip of green crepe ¾-inch wide. Paste it in place at the base of the calyx, and placing two No. 9 wires, 15-inches long beside the

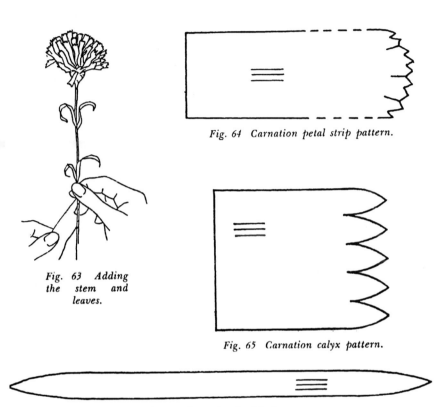

Fig. 64   *Carnation petal strip pattern.*

Fig. 63   *Adding the stem and leaves.*

Fig. 65   *Carnation calyx pattern.*

Fig. 66   *Carnation leaf pattern.*

short stems formed by the spool wire, start wrapping all as one stem. About 2½-inches below the base of the flower, wrap in the first leaf. Bend the leaf in half across the center. Hold the folded end close to the stem and wrap the folded end in with the stem so that the two pointed ends flare out from the stem (*Fig. 63*). Proceed in the same way with the other leaves wrapping them in on opposite sides of the stem about 2½-inches apart. After the leaves are inserted, curl[5] them back over a scissors blade. The carnation is now ready for display.

See General Direction 7, *p.* 227; 8, *p.* 227; 9, *p.* 227; 5, *p.* 225

Apple Blossoms

Fig. 67 Apple blossom.

IT'S NICE TO know how to make apple blossoms for, symbolic of spring, they are favorites for spring party trims, school proms, lodge dances and banquets and they are also widely used for store windows. (See Chapter XIV on How to Make Money with Paper Crafts.)

The directions below tell how to make stems and branches as well as blossoms. When masses are needed for trimming dance halls, stages, etc. only the blossoms need be made. They can be tied to natural branches.

Materials Needed to Make Four Sprays:

    1 fold crepe paper white for inside of petals
    1 fold crepe paper pink for outside of petals
    1 fold crepe paper yellow for centers
    1 fold crepe paper light green for leaves
    1 fold crepe paper darker green for leaves
    1 fold crepe paper brown for branches
    2 spools No. 1 or 2 wire
    4 No. 7 wires
    2 No. 15 wires
    Paste, cardboard, tissue paper, wire cutters or pliers

NOTE: *Duplex crepe (one side pink, the other white) may be used for the blossoms and also (in two shades of green) for the leaves. Ready-made rose stamens may replace yellow crepe for the centers. Three bunches are needed for four sprays. These directions are for one spray with three branches and about thirty-two blossoms. Both No. 7 and 15 wires are specified above. If your dealer doesn't have both sizes you can use either the 7 or 15, though both are better.*

Step 1. Make the Patterns.[12] The outlines for the petals, leaves and calyx are shown in Figures 73, 74, 75.

Step 2. Cut the Petals, Leaves, Calyx, Centers and Buds. From pink crepe cut strips of petals,[13] making about 160 petals. Cut the strips into sections, five petals to each. Cut the same number of white petals and paste them together.[10]

Cut sixteen leaves of Duplex crepe, or thirty-two of two shades of green and paste them together.[10]

For the calyx, cut forty-one from the light green crepe (one for each flower and nine buds).

For the buds, cut nine 5-inch squares and nine 3-inch squares of pink crepe.

For the centers, cut a strip [1] of light yellow crepe 1-inch wide and 18-inches long.

Fig. 68 Apple blossom bud.

Fig. 69 Apple blossom with ready-made stamens.

Fig. 70 Bud with calyx.

Step 3. Prepare the Petals, Buds and Stamens. Flute [3] each petal once in the center top, and cup [4] each about one third from the top. Hold the white side up as you cup. To make the buds crush one of the 5-inch squares of crepe into a ball about ½-inch in diameter. Stretch one of the 3-inch squares and drape it over the ball pinching it together under the ball (*Fig. 68*). To prepare the stamens, stretch your 18-inch strip. Along one edge cut it into fringe ½-inch deep.[2] Cut this into ¾-inch lengths. Gather each into a little bunch and hold it together at the bottom with a bit of paste. (If you're using ready-made stamens, fold six for each blossom—in two.)

Step 4. Put the Blossoms Together (*Fig. 69*). Gather a petal strip (white side up) around a center with the petals overlapping. Tie [6] at the

See General Direction 12, *p.* 229; 13, *p.* 229; 10, *p.* 228; 1, *p.* 223; 3, *p.* 224; 4, *p.* 224; 2, *p.* 223; 6, *p.* 226

base with a 7-inch length of spool wire. Put a little paste on the band of the calyx and arrange it around the base of the blossom, turning the points outward. Vary your flowers so that they won't look as though they had been stamped from a machine. On a few

Fig. 71 Bouquet of blossoms and buds.

use only one, two or three petals—as though some had drifted away; on a few omit the calyx. Wrap[7] the stem with a ½-inch wide strip of light green crepe. Paste a calyx around each bud (*Fig. 70*). Vary these, too. On some, let the points come up around the bud, on others let the points stand out as though the bud were opening. Using

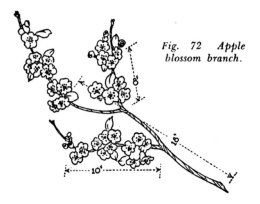

Fig. 72 Apple blossom branch.

the surplus crepe at the base of the bud as a stem, wrap it with a ½-inch wide strip of light green crepe. Make a little bouquet of four or five blossoms and three or four buds. About 2-inches from the blossoms, start wrapping all the stems together, using a strip of green ¾-inch wide. Insert two leaves at the beginning, on opposite sides of the stem. (*Fig. 71*)[9]

_____

See General Direction 7, *p.* 227; 9, *p.* 227

Step 5. Make Three Branches. Cut a No. 7 wire into three stems, one 8-, one 10-, one 18-inches long. Wrap each one with brown crepe paper, 1-inch wide. If possible wrap a real twig in at the end. Rewrap, this time inserting the little clusters of blossoms and buds.[9] On the shortest wire, add the blossom clusters about 4-inches apart; on the other two, about 5-inches apart.

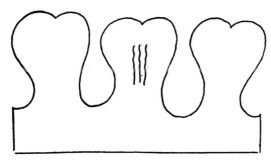

Fig. 73 Apple blossom petal strip pattern.

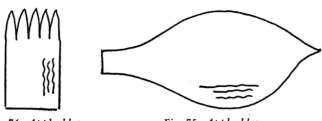

Fig. 74 Apple blos-
som calyx pattern.

Fig. 75 Apple blos-
som leaf pattern.

Step 6. Join the Branches to Make a Spray (*Fig. 72*). When all three branches are put together, join them in one big branch. To do that, use a No. 15 wire as a base. Wrap and rewrap it with brown crepe paper. Use a wide strip of brown crepe, 2-inches doubled to 1-inch. Before the wire is quite thick enough insert the three branches. If making up several sprays, arrange each one differently.

See General Direction 9, *p.* 227

Pompons

Fig. 76 Pompon.

PERHAPS YOU'D RATHER design your own flowers than copy nature's. There's little to limit you in such designing. Shapes, sizes, coloring may be fantastic or they may be reminiscent of nature's specimens. The pompon is one such make-believe.

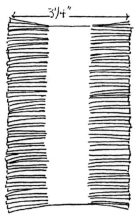

Fig. 77 Pompon fringe strip. The fringe is cut 1¼-inches deep.

Materials Needed to Make One Dozen:
 1 fold crepe paper desired color for flowers
 1 fold crepe paper leafy green for leaves and stem
 1 spool wire No. 1 or 2
 6 wires No. 7
 Paste

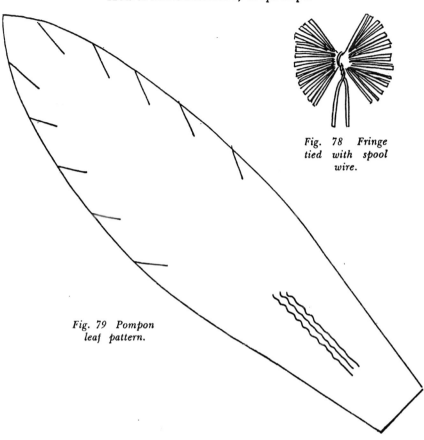

Fig. 78 Fringe
tied with spool
wire.

Fig. 79 Pompon
leaf pattern.

Cut a strip[1] of crepe paper $3\frac{1}{4}$-inches wide and 36-inches long. This makes a medium size flower, about like a big carnation. Stretch the strip slightly and then cut each edge along its entire length into fringe[2] about $1\frac{1}{4}$-inches deep (*Fig. 77*). Gather, do not roll, the strip through the center with your fingers, and tie[6] it tightly with a 10-inch length of spool wire (*Fig. 78*). Now shape the little bundle with your hands to give a pompon look—pushing the fringed ends together. Brush the surface with the palm of your hands to round it off, and if you think it's needed, trim off some of the uneven ends. If you want a fatter flower, put two together. From there on, proceed to wrap the stem adding in whatever foliage you like.[7,8,9] A satisfactory leaf pattern is given in Figure 79.

See General Direction 1, *p.* 223; 2, *p.* 223; 6, *p.* 226; 7, *p.* 227; 8, *p.* 227; 9, *p.* 227

Easter Lilies

Fig. 80   Easter lily.

THESE DIRECTIONS ARE for a plant of three flowers and two buds.

Materials Needed to Make One Plant:
  1 fold crepe paper white for petals
  1 fold crepe paper yellow for stamens
  1 fold crepe paper light green for pistils
  1 fold crepe paper leafy green for leaves
  1 spool wire No. 1
  6 No. 10 wires
  2 wires No. 7
  Paste, tissue paper, cardboard or wrapping paper

NOTE: *White Duplex crepe is pleasant for making petals and green Duplex for the leaves. However, if you can't buy it, don't worry; single crepe is entirely satisfactory.*

Step 1. Make the Patterns.[12] The outlines for petals and leaves are shown in Figures 86 and 87.

Step 2. Cut the Flowers, Buds, Leaves.[13] Cut eighteen leaves; three flowers and two buds. In cutting the flower, be sure to place your pattern so that the grain of the crepe runs as indicated by the three short lines. For the buds, use one-half (three points) of the pattern for each.

Step 3. Prepare the Parts. For the petals, cut six No. 10 wires into 7½-inch lengths. Wrap each one with a ¼-inch wide strip of white crepe paper.[7] Paste one wire [11] down the center of each petal on the shiny side of the crepe (*Fig. 81*). With the wires on the outside, paste the two sides of the flower together. To prepare the buds,

See General Direction 12, *p.* 229; 13, *p.* 229; 7, *p.* 227; 11, *p.* 229

[38]

paste the two sides together, then paste the petal tips together. Tie [6] the buds at the base, 2-inches from the bottom, with a 10-inch length of spool wire.

For the pistil, the center of the flower (*Fig. 82*), cut a 5-inch length of spool wire. Bend 1-inch at one end to form a loop. Wrap [7] the

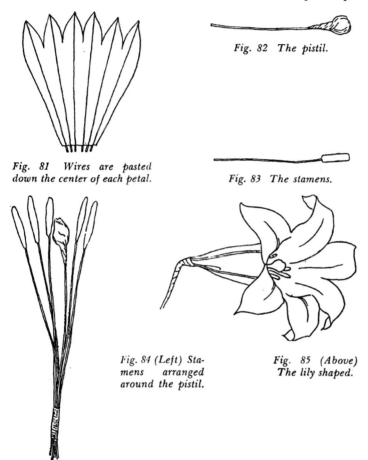

Fig. 82 The pistil.

Fig. 81 Wires are pasted down the center of each petal.

Fig. 83 The stamens.

Fig. 84 (Left) Stamens arranged around the pistil.

Fig. 85 (Above) The lily shaped.

½-inch loop or wire about 10 times with a strip of light green crepe cut ½-inch wide. Wrap the remaining wire to the end. The stamens (*Fig. 83*) are made by cutting five pieces of spool wire, 5-inches long. Wind each with a strip of yellow crepe cut ½-inch wide, wrapping the tips three or four times to make them thick. Arrange the

See General Direction 6, *p.* 226; 7, *p.* 227

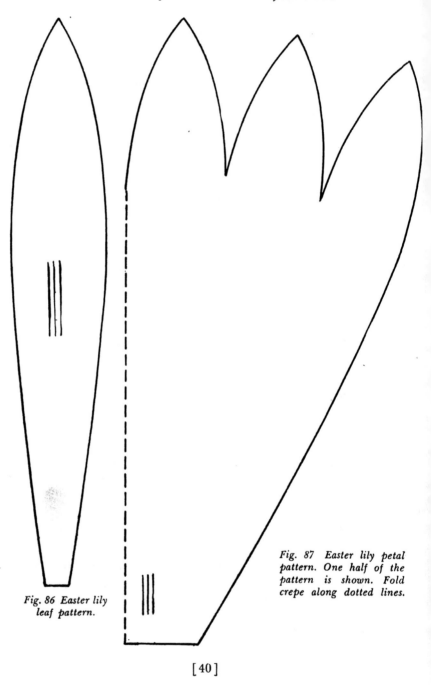

Fig. 86 Easter lily leaf pattern.

Fig. 87 Easter lily petal pattern. One half of the pattern is shown. Fold crepe along dotted lines.

stamens around the pistil (*Fig. 84*) and wrap them together at the base with a ½-inch wide strip of light green crepe.

Step 4. Add the Stems to Flowers and Buds. Cut the following wires: Five pieces of spool wire 10-inches long; five of No. 7, 6-inches long; one of No. 7, 10-inches long and one No. 7, 20 inches long. Place a center—pistil and stamens—inside each flower. The wires of the center should be even with the base of the flower. Tie the flower together 1-inch from the base with a 10-inch length of spool wire. Wrap the wire with a strip of green crepe ½-inch wide, adding a No. 7 wire [8] 6-inches long. Wrap the stems of the buds in the same way adding a No. 7 wire 6-inches long.

Step 5. Assemble the Plant.[7,8,9] The main stem is the 20-inch No. 7 wire. To this, flowers, buds and leaves are added at attractive intervals. Ten inches from the bottom of the stem, the 10-inch No. 7 wire is added for reinforcement. In wrapping, place one bud at the tip of the main stem. Use a strip of green crepe 1-inch wide for wrapping the main stem.

Step 6. Shape the Flowers and Leaves. Curl the petals back with your fingers (*Fig. 85*); curl [5] the leaves over your scissors blade. Bend your flowers at right angles to the stem and the lily is ready for the holidays.

These lovely tulips were made according to the directions on Page 8.

See General Direction 8, *p.* 227; 7, *p.* 227; 9, *p.* 227; 5, *p.* 225

Fig. 88 Pond lily.

Pond Lilies

HERE'S A FLOWER you can take liberties with! Make it in any color you like. It's pretty in all the pastels and in many vivid colors as well as in white. Tint its petals near the base; make it three times normal size if you wish a dramatic flower to overflow a low bowl, and—finally, wax it if you like. Nature designed it in such a conventional pattern that no one is shocked if nature's colors and sizes are over-emphasized.

Materials Needed to Make One Dozen:

    1 fold crepe paper, say white, for petals
    1 fold crepe paper, soft yellow, for center
    1 fold crepe paper, pale green, for center
    1 fold crepe paper, leaf green, for leaves and stems
    1 No. 2 spool wire
    2 dozen No. 9 wire
    Paste, tissue paper, cardboard or wrapping paper

NOTE: *For the petals, Duplex crepe can be used in place of the single white. White with pink or pale yellow is pretty. Green Duplex can be used for the leaves.*

Step 1. Make the Patterns.[12] The outlines for petals and leaves are shown in Figures 93 and 94.

Step 2. Make the Center (*Fig. 89*). First crush a wad of pale green paper into a ball about ½-inch in diameter. Cut a 2½-inch square of the same green, stretch it, and cover the ball with it, pinching the

See General Direction 12, *p.* 229

crepe together underneath the ball. Flatten the top of the ball slightly. Cut a 2-inch wide strip [1] of soft yellow crepe. Cut it along one edge into fine fringe [2] about 1½-inches deep. Curl [5] the fringed ends over a scissors blade. Cut the strip into 10-inch lengths. Gather a strip around the ball center (*Fig. 90*) and tie [6] it in place with spool wire. Note in Fig. 90 that the fringe curls in, and that the ends are high above the ball center.

Fig. 89 Pond lily center.

Fig. 90 Completing the center.

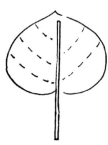

Fig. 91 Leaf wired.

Fig. 92 Arranging the petals around the center.

Step 3. Cut the Petals, Calyx, Leaves.[13] Cut 30 petals for each flower. For the calyx cut a 4-inch wide strip [1] of pale green and leaf green crepe. Cut four petals from each color to make each calyx. Paste one of each color together.[10] Cut two or more leaves for each flower. Note that the grain of the crepe runs across the leaf. The leaves should be of double thickness. If you do not have green Duplex crepe, cut twice as many leaves as you need.

Step 4. Prepare the Parts. Cup [4] twelve petals deeply toward the top. Do this with the "wrong" or shiny side of the paper toward you. Cup nine slightly less deeply. Cup the remaining nine even less. Cup toward the top each "petal" that forms the calyx, light green side

See General Direction 1, *p.* 223; 2, *p.* 223; 5, *p.* 225; 6, *p.* 226; 13, *p.* 229; 10, *p.* 228; 4, *p.* 224

Fig. 93 Pond lily leaf pattern.

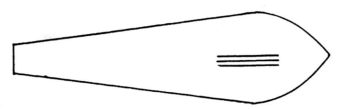

Fig. 94 Pond lily petal and calyx pattern.

up. Cup these moderately. For each leaf, cut a 6-inch length of No. 9 wire. Wrap [7] it three times with a strip of leaf green crepe cut ¾-inch wide. Paste the wire down the center length of the leaf (*Fig. 91*).[11] If you are using single crepe, paste another leaf over the first one, applying the paste over the entire leaf. When paste has partially dried, draw in veins with your fingernail or a knitting needle.

See General Direction 7, *p.* 227; 11, *p.* 229

Step 5. Put the Flower Together. Arrange the twelve deeply cupped petals around the center first. The tips of the petals should lie a good inch above the center. Hold each petal in place at the base with a bit of paste. As you arrange them, row after row, overlap the petals, and see to it that the petal points in each row come between those of the preceding row. Arrange next the nine petals that are moderately cupped, and last, the nine that are cupped the least. From the beginning around the center, each succeeding row will require less and less overlapping till on the final rows there will be no overlapping at all.

Tie [6] the petals, when all are arranged, with two No. 9 wires, 15-inches long.

Paste the four petals that form the calyx around the base of the flower. Paste them at even intervals.

Step 6. Add the Stem and Leaves.[7,8,9] Cut two 15-inch lengths of No. 9 or No. 10 wire. Start wrapping the flower at its base with a strip of leaf green crepe, cut $\frac{3}{4}$-inch wide. Insert the two stem wires and proceed with the wrapping inserting the two leaves on opposite sides of the stem near the flower. Rewrap the stem to make it thicker and smoother. Bend it into a spiral so the lily will appear to float in a shallow bowl.

HOW TO WAX CREPE PAPER FLOWERS

WAXED PAPER FLOWERS enjoy periods of popularity. Now they're in style, now they're out. In or out, a bowl of mixed flowers smoothly waxed can have a certain Victorian charm, and a bouquet beautifully waxed can always stop crowds in front of the most expensive florist shop window in any big city. Pond lilies are perennial waxed favorites. If the moment comes, when you'd like to wax some of the crepe paper flowers you've made, it will be handy to know how. So we give you here two easy wax solutions. The method of application is the same for both.

Wax Solutions for Paper Flowers:

Solution 1. Table candles melted. Odds and ends even in different colors as long as they are all pale shades may be melted together. White is best for leaves and stems.

Solution 2. 4 pounds of Parawax, 4 ounces of Spermaceti, $\frac{1}{2}$ of a Plumber's Candle.

Method of Application:

First make your flowers. Complete them to the last detail for this is a process of total immersion. The two-toned effect of Duplex crepe is somewhat lost in the waxing process, but Duplex is often

---

See General Direction 6, *p.* 226; 7, *p.* 227; 8, *p.* 227; 9, *p.* 227

used because of its thickness. Single crepe, however, is entirely satisfactory. Flowers with large independent petals are the easiest and most satisfactory to wax. White flowers that have been tinted with "Pastello" crayons turn out beautifully.

Place your ingredients in a double boiler. In working with wax over a stove take every precaution against starting a fire. It must never reach the smoking hot stage. When the candles have melted, remove the wicks with a fork. The wax must be deep enough to cover the flowers when you dip them. Bring the ingredients to a temperature of 130 degrees. If you don't have a thermometer, test the mixture by dipping a piece of crepe paper in and out of the kettle quickly. If the crepe retains its freshness and a fine transparent coating of the wax, the temperature is right. If the paper shrivels up, obviously the heat is too much for it. When the test is satisfactory, turn off the heat and, holding the flower by its stem, dip it into and out of the solution quickly. Shake the flower carefully over the kettle to remove any excess wax. If any has lodged in the center of the flower, remove it with an orange stick or a tooth pick. If the petals have stuck together, separate them gently and reshape them if necessary.

Let the wax set for about ten minutes. Then repeat the process. After that you can dip the flower as many times as necessary to get the finish you like. The melted materials should be slightly cooler with each dipping, about 120 degrees (no less) for the final immersion. While the wax is soft, care must be taken to place the flower upright so there will be no pressure against it.

If you wish, you may dip the leaves and the entire stem too; or, you may coat them by spooning the heated liquid over them, or you may leave the stem and leaves free of wax.

Dogwood takes time to make but it rewards you. This particular spray is waxed.

[46]

CHAPTER II

How to Make Decorations and Favors for "Once=in=a=Lifetime" Events

FLOWERS AND CANDLES won't do for parties celebrating the big moments in life. Such occasions call for decorations designed specifically for them. Engagement announcements, showers for brides, showers for babies, anniversaries, children's birthday parties—all these call for very special decorations—decorations which you can make yourself, for yourself, for your friends, or for shops selling party decorations.

FOUR WAYS TO ANNOUNCE AN ENGAGEMENT AT A PARTY

A PRETTY SURPRISE to break the news to those supposedly unsuspecting guests adds gaiety to an engagement party. Here are four light-hearted suggestions.

In the Heart of a Rose

Provide one rose for each guest. Tie the short stem with a bow of florist's ribbon. See Page 106 for making professional bows. In the center of each rose, tuck a tiny card bearing the names of the bride-and-groom to be. If the announcement is made at a "stand-up" tea, pass a large silver tray heaped with the roses; if it's made at a dinner party, place one of the roses on each service plate.

Gardenias to You

If the announcement is made at a party for the future bride's girl friends, follow the same idea given above, but tie the announcement card to the stem of an artificial gardenia. You can make these according to the directions on Page 12. Each guest may take hers home as a pretty and wearable little gift.

By Candlelight

At each place at a dinner party or a luncheon, put a prettily iced cup cake on a white paper lace doily. In the center of each, stick a wee rose bud candleholder (*Fig. 1*). In the holder place a candle size roll of white paper tied daintily with a satin ribbon and bow. See Page 106. Inside each roll write the names of the future bride and groom. This announcement can also serve as a place card. In front of each cake place a card bearing the guest's name.

Fig. 1 (Left) Candle-light announcement (approx. 2-inches high).

Fig. 2 (Right) Two hearts announcement (approx. 2-inches high).

Two Hearts That Beat as One

On a large mint patty (*Fig. 2*), pastel colored, stick the tips of two hearts cut from contrasting pastel colored cardboard. Overlap the hearts, and across them paste a gold Cupid's arrow. On one heart, write the name of the bride-to-be, on the other the groom's. Place the mint on a white paper lace doily, and attach a place card to it with a satin ribbon and bow.

TABLE DECORATIONS FOR THE ENGAGEMENT PARTY

Two Hearts United—A Centerpiece

Figure 3 illustrates a romantic centerpiece for this memorable occasion.

Fig. 3 Engagement party centerpiece (approx. 12-inches high).

The two hearts are made of silver paper. At the top they are tied with a pink maline bow through which is tucked a cluster of pastel colored flowers. The hearts are nested in four pastel ruffles of crepe paper. Huge bows of the pink maline give additional froth to the base.

This centerpiece can also be used for breaking the news of the engagement. Tiny pink hearts bearing the names of the couple to be married can be tucked in between the ruffles. Each heart should have a long satin ribbon tied to it. At the opposite end of the ribbons, placed at the guests' plates, place cards should be attached.

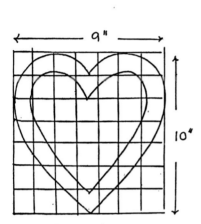

Fig. 4   Outline for "two hearts" centerpiece.

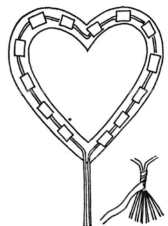

Fig. 5   Cardboard heart reinforced with wire.

Materials Needed to Make One Centerpiece:

1 box about 10½-inches square and 2-inches deep

1 sheet silver wrapping paper, enough to cut out four hearts about 9 by 10-inches

Light weight cardboard, 9 by 10-inches (office correspondence files are perfect)

6 yards maline ribbon, 4-inches wide

4 yards maline ribbon, 2-inches wide

Crepe paper

1 spool wire No. 1

6 wires No. 10

6 wires No. 7 or 15

Paste, gummed paper tape, 2 wire shanks

NOTE: *Any four or five pastel shades of crepe paper may be used. Pale green and yellow should be included, unless you prefer to tie in a sprig of fresh rather than artificial flowers at the top.*

Step 1. Cut out four silver hearts and four cardboard hearts. A small outline is given in Figure 4. Enlarge this to 9-by-10-inches. An easy way to do that is to cut a piece of wrapping paper 9-by-10-inches. Rule it off into the same number of squares shown on the outline. Take your pencil and draw in the heart shape square by square.

Step 2. Paste the silver hearts over the cardboard ones.

Step 3. Reinforce the hearts. Even though your hearts are of four thicknesses of paper, they will be wobbly unless you strengthen them. To do that gum tape a No. 7 or 15 wire down the center of two of the cardboard hearts (*Fig. 5*). Where the wires meet at the hearts' tips, leave ends of 6-inches. Over each wired heart, paste an unwired one.

Step 4. Wrap [7] the wire ends together. Include with the ends four 6-inch lengths of No. 15 wire. Do your wrapping with a strip [1] of crepe paper 1½-inches wide, cut from the color of the crepe selected for your top ruffle. Paste your strip down at the tip of the hearts and wrap them firmly for 2-inches, then paste down and cut off the strip.

Step 5. Punch a hole in the center of the box lid. Poke the unwrapped wires through the hole. Spread them out on the under side of the box and gum tape them down. These operations are necessary to hold the hearts upright.

Step 6. Fasten hearts together. Where they overlap, fasten them together with wire shanks.

Step 7. Make ruffles for base. Cut four strips [1] of paper, from four different pastel shades, right across the entire fold. Cut the first or bottom one 9-inches wide; the next 7½; the next 6; the last 4½. Open up the strips and from the one to be used for the bottom ruffle cut off about a yard. Using the longer length, fold and refold it to eight thicknesses. Along one side, cut the eight layers into scallops about 2-inches wide. They don't have to be accurately cut. On the sewing machine or by hand gather the opposite edge, then paste it down around the base of the hearts. Gather and paste in place each of the ruffles.

Step 8. Make a small cluster of flowers for the center top. Use the patterns for the apple blossoms, Page 35, and leaves of the carnation, Page 31. Cut the flowers from assorted pastel colors. Directions for making apple blossoms are on Page 32. It isn't necessary to make stems. The spool wire used to tie the base of the flowers is sufficient.

Step 9. Make Maline Bows and Tie in Place. Tie a bow of several loops from the narrow maline for the top, catching in the cluster of

See General Direction 7, *p.* 227; 1, *p.* 223

flowers. Tie it to the connected hearts with spool wire. Make several large bows of the wide maline and with spool wire tie them to the base of the hearts. See Page 106 for making bows.

Nut Cup in a Heart

This cup (*Fig. 6*) can be made from material left over from the Two Hearts United Centerpiece. The only additional purchase you need make are the nut cups themselves. Get the smallest size you can find. Officially known as souffle cups, they are sold in some department, stationery and chain stores.

*Fig. 6 Nut cup
in a heart.*

Step 1. Make the Hearts. From your silver wrapping paper scraps, cut out hearts using the outline given on Page 49. If your silver paper is limp, paste it on to heavy white paper. Make a paper circular pattern a trifle larger than the base of your souffle cup. From each heart cut a hole the size of the circle.

Step 2. Cover the Nut Cups. Cut crepe paper, say pink, across the grain ½-inch wider than the height of your cups. Brush the outside of the cup very lightly with paste. Around the cup and its rim stretch the crepe strip so tightly that the top edge of the crepe will lie curled ¼-inch or more inside the cup. Remember that the rougher side of the crepe paper is the right side. Trim the crepe strip evenly at the bottom if necessary.

Step 3. Fasten Blossom and Bow. Fasten a paper flower and small maline bow to the edge of the cup. The easiest way is to punch a pin size hole in the side of the cup, put a 2-inch length of white spool wire through it and tie the bow in place with the wire. Twist, don't knot the wire. Cut off the surplus ends.

Step 4. Slip cup through heart.
The finished product is now ready to grace your table.

[51]

PRETTY SHOWERS FOR THE BRIDE-TO-BE

MR. WEBSTER may say that a shower is a "party given to a prospective bride where gifts are presented," but to most of us something must be added to that definition. The gifts must be presented in an attractive way. Fancy parasols and watering cans are very popular.

A Transparent Parasol for a Bridal Shower

The easiest way to achieve a pretty shower parasol is to trim a clear transparent umbrella.

No step-by-step directions are necessary, for you don't have to make anything; you merely bedeck the parasol with ribbons and flowers.

Fig. 7 (Upper right) Transparent parasol trimmed for bridal shower. Fig. 8 (Above) Crepe paper parasol for bridal shower.

The one sketched (*Fig. 7*) is trimmed like this. To the edge of the umbrella, ruffles of paper lace doilies are attached with strips of transparent Scotch tape. The ruffles are the borders cut off round doilies. That's why they have such a perky flare. Pale blue satin ribbon is held in loops with small patches of Scotch tape. Pink crepe paper roses are held in place in the same way. The top of the parasol is bedecked in similar fashion and by the same means. . . . The handle is wrapped spirally with pink ribbon. Ungainly spokes are wrapped with pink crepe paper cut in ½-inch wide strips across the grain.

[52]

How to Make a Shower Parasol

The photo (*Fig. 8*) shows as pretty a parasol as one could dream of. One or two on a luncheon table with daintily wrapped gift packages near by make a superlatively attractive table.

What's important, too, is that this concoction is easy and inexpensive to make.

Materials Needed to Make One Parasol:

1 fold crepe paper

> Use pink or blue or pale green for a spring bride; yellow, turquoise or even one of the darker colors such as rich green or ruby red for a fall bride if you are not timid about breaking with convention.

1 sheet medium weight cardboard, 13 by 26-inches.

> Enough to cut two circles 13-inches in diameter.

1 round wooden stick about 18-inches long, and 1/4-inch in diameter for the handle of the parasol.

> A dowel stick will serve the purpose.

1 wire No. 7 or 15

1 spool wire No. 1 or 2 (optional)

3 yards satin baby ribbon

> Use white ribbon if you're covering the parasol with a light pastel crepe; use a matching or blending ribbon with one of the deeper shades of crepe.

Paste, gummed paper tape

NOTE: *The parasol itself is made of two layers of cardboard. The upper one conceals wires pasted to the top of the lower. The wires hold the handle in place.*

Step 1. Make pattern for the parasol. From wrapping paper cut a 13-inch circle. Cut out an inverted V or pie-piece section 4-inches wide at the base (*Fig. 9*).

Step 2. Using your pattern as a guide, cut two shapes from light weight cardboard.

Step 3. Cut three 15-inch squares of crepe paper.

Step 4. Cover your two cardboard shapes with crepe paper. Do it in this way: Brush a border of paste about 1/4-inch wide around the edges and the inverted V opening of your shapes. Lay the crepe paper squares over them. Press the edges down carefully. Cut away all the surplus crepe. On one of the shapes, add—in the same way—a second layer of crepe paper. This shape forms the top of the parasol. One layer of crepe can be used, but two give a richer look.

[53]

Step 5. Form parasols of the shapes by overlapping the sides of the inverted V, and pasting them together. One shape will form the top of the parasol, the other the lining. On the latter, the crepe paper lies on the inside.

Step 6. Wrap [7] the handle once with a ¾-inch wide strip [1] of crepe paper.

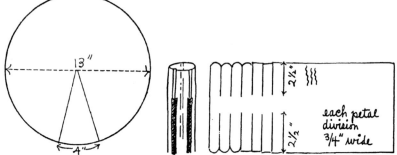

Fig. 9 Diagram for making parasol.   *Fig. 10 Wires gum taped to parasol handle.*   *Fig. 11 Diagram for cutting the petal strips.*

Step 7. Cut three 8-inch lengths of No. 7 or 15 wire (*Fig. 10*). Gum tape them firmly to one end of the handle with their ends even with the end of the handle, and spaced at even intervals around the handle. Most important, tape them beginning at their bottom ends for 5-inches only. Note Figure 10.

Step 8. Cut a small hole in the top of the cardboard parasol (the one that forms the lining). Thrust the wired end of the handle through it so that 3-inches extend above the top.

Step 9. Bend the three wires down and fasten them to the outside of the cardboard with patches of gummed paper tape.

Step 10. Brush the top of the cardboard with paste.

Step 11. Put on the top of your parasol. Cut a hole in the center top, so you can drop the parasol into place.

Step 12. Cut four 6-inch lengths of baby ribbon. Paste one end of each to the top of the parasol, spacing them evenly around it. Draw the ends down toward the bottom and paste them lightly in place. To the center of the ribbons, paste tiny bows.

Step 13. Prepare the trimming. Twisted petals are used around the edge and to make the pompon-like ornaments on the handles. There are three of them. The one that doesn't show in the sketch, but does when the parasol lies on the table, is at the top of the handle on the inside of the parasol. Cut strips of crepe paper

See General Direction 7, *p.* 227; 1, *p.* 223

6-inches wide across the grain. Then cut the strip along each side into a petal strip (*Fig. 11*). Open up the strip and twist [18] the petals. Make your twists deep and complete, mild little twirling won't give the lush effect needed.

Step 14. Make Ruffle. A very full ruffle can be made from one strip to paste around the edge of the parasol. Gather it through its center length on the machine and paste it with the lower edge of the petals just a bit lower than the lower edge of the parasol. Tie or paste very full ruffles of the petals to the top of the handle; toward the bottom of it; and to the top inside the parasol. (If you wish, make these ruffles over a ruler, and tie them in place with spool wire.)

Step 15. Tie a ribbon bow with long streamers to the handle. The parasol is now complete.

A Glamorized Watering Can Holds Gifts for the Bride-to-Be

This traditional favorite (*Fig. 12*) for "showering" the bride is given trousseau daintiness with ruffles and bows and silver ribbons.

Fig. 12 Watering can gift holder (approx. 7-inches from base to hood).

Materials Needed to Make One Watering Can:

2 folds crepe paper, pastel colors

or

1 fold crepe paper and
1 sheet white glazed paper

1 sheet cardboard

See General Direction 18, *p.* 232

1 wire No. 7 or 15
1 spool wire No. 1
4 wire shanks
3 yards narrow satin ribbon
1¼-yards silver paper ribbon ½-inch wide
Gummed paper tape, paste, wire cutters or pliers

NOTE: *Optional materials are a spray of artificial flowers and one roll of clear cellophane for the rain from the spout. The white glazed wrapping paper is also known as "Flint Glazed Paper." This material, which shines like oil cloth, can be found in many departments that carry gift wrapping papers. It makes a pretty covering, and one easy to use, for the can and its spout. Crepe paper can be used but it requires a little "know-how" which is covered in these directions.*

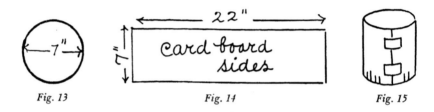

| Fig. 13 | Fig. 14 | Fig. 15 |

Step 1. Cut circle 7-inches across, from cardboard (*Fig. 13*).

Step 2. Cut strip of cardboard (*Fig. 14*).

Step 3. Hold bottom and sides together with small patches of gummed tape (*Fig. 15*).

Step 4. Cut crepe paper lining. The three wavy lines indicate the grain of the crepe (*Fig. 16*).

Step 5. Paste lining to top, outside of can (*Fig. 17*).

Step 6. Turn crepe paper down over the top to cover the inside (*Fig. 18*).

Step 7. Cut strip of crepe paper, or white glazed for the outside covering (*Fig. 19*).

Step 8. Cut a strip of cardboard (*Fig. 20*). This is for the hood. Wrap it with a strip of crepe paper cut 2-inches wide. Make a ruffle 1½-inches wide, gathered down center length on the machine. Paste it lightly along the gathers to the cardboard.

Step 9. Cut a strip of crepe paper for the hood (*Fig. 21*).

Step 10. Paste the cardboard strip across the crepe paper ¾-inch from edge (*Fig. 22*).

Step 11. Flute the ¾-inch edge. Note Figure 22.

Step 12. Fasten the hood to the can at sides with wire shanks. Paste crepe down at back and sides, gathering it in where necessary.

Step 13. Cover the can. Brush it lightly with paste and cover it with crepe paper or white glazed paper.

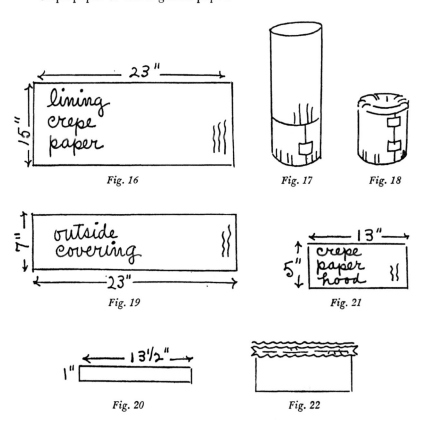

Fig. 16 *Fig. 17* *Fig. 18*

Fig. 19 *Fig. 21*

Fig. 20 *Fig. 22*

Step 14. Make handle (*Fig. 23*). Cut a cardboard strip. Down its center length fasten No. 7 or 15 wire with bits of gummed paper tape.

Step 15. Cover handle. First wrap it with a strip of crepe paper 2-inches wide. Then make a ruffle 1½-inches wide, 29-inches long, gathered through the center length. Paste it lightly along the gathers to the handle.

Step 16. With wire shanks, fasten the handle in place (*Fig. 24*).

Step 17. Make spout (*Fig. 25*). Roll a piece of cardboard, 6-by-9¾-inches into a tube 9¾-inches long and 1½-inches in diameter. Paste the sides together. Cover spout with crepe or white glazed paper. Grain

[57]

of crepe must run from top to base of spout. Cut one end of spout to a slant, making the shorter side 8¾-inches long. Cut cardboard circle for other end of spout 2-inches across. Cover it with crepe paper and paste it to end of spout. If you wish to add "rain" to spout, slash clear transparent Cellophane into long fringe. Tie it at one end with ribbon and bow. Paste ribbon to cardboard circle.

Step 18. Fasten spout to can. Slash longer side of slanted end into tabs about 1-inch deep (*Fig. 26*). Bend tabs at right angles and paste spout to can.

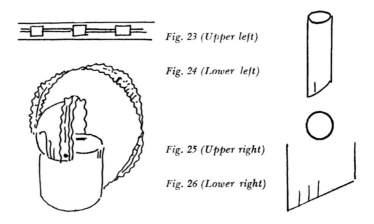

Fig. 23 (*Upper left*)

Fig. 24 (*Lower left*)

Fig. 25 (*Upper right*)

Fig. 26 (*Lower right*)

Step 19. Make two ruffles for bottom of can. Cut one 4-inches wide. Stitch silver paper ribbon along one edge. Gather the opposite edge. Paste it around the bottom of the can ½-inch from the edge. Cut other ruffle 3-inches wide. Gather it down center length. Paste it to outside bottom of can.

Step 20. Decorate the can with ribbon bows. See Chapter IV for tying bows. A spray of artificial flowers may be added.

Step 21. Make ruffle for top edge of can. Cut strip of crepe paper 2-inches wide. Gather it down center length, and paste it in place along the gathers. When this is done, the gifts can be piled in the can.

Parasol Nut Cups

Dainty nut cups add surprisingly to the festive appearance of the luncheon or dinner table. Without rivals for popularity are wee Watering Can Nut Cups and tiny Parasol Nut Cups. Figure 27 shows a quick

[58]

and inexpensive way to make Parasol cups. Pretty in assorted colors!

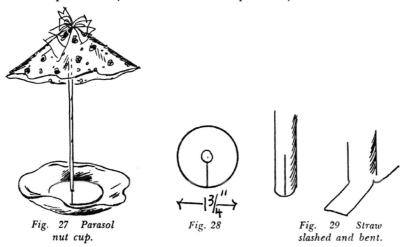

Fig. 27 *Parasol*
nut cup.

Fig. 28

Fig. 29 *Straw*
slashed and bent.

Materials Needed to Make One Dozen:

1 fold Duplex crepe paper pastel color
1 sheet tissue paper pastel color
Scraps of cardboard
6 soda straws
5 yards baby ribbon
Paste

Step 1. Cut circle of Duplex crepe 3¾-inches in diameter. With your fingers, stretch it to cup shape.

Step 2. Cut circle of cardboard, 1¾-inches in diameter.

Step 3. Cut circle 1¾-inches of Duplex and slash it in one place from the edge to the center. Cut a little hole there (*Fig. 28*). (The straw handle fits in it later.)

Step 4. Cut soda straw in half.

Step 5. With fine scissors make two slashes 1-inch deep in one end of the straw. Spread the slashed ends out flat (*Fig. 29*).

Step 6. Cut 3½-inch circle of pastel tissue paper. If possible use pinking shears.

Step 7. Put a dab of paste in center of tissue paper and pinch the circle down on top of the straw. Paste a wee bow of ribbon to top of parasol. See Page 106 for tying bows.

Step 8. Paste the parasol to the cardboard circle by covering the circle with paste and pressing on to it the bent back tabs.

Step 9. Place the smaller circle of Duplex over the pasted cardboard.

Step 10. Paste the cardboard circle inside the cup shaped circle of Duplex. After the paste is dry they are ready for use.

Watering Can Nut Cup

This cup (*Fig. 30*) is the all-time favorite for a bridal shower.

Fig. 30 (Left) Watering can nut cup.

Fig. 31 (Right) "Hood" for watering can nut cup.

Materials Needed to Make One Dozen:
   1 fold crepe paper pastel color
   6 yards narrow satin ribbon white or pastel
   12 souffle cups
   Paste

NOTE: *Souffle Cup is the official name for the nut cup forms.*

Step 1. Make the "hood" (*Fig. 31*) of the watering can by cutting across the grain of the crepe a strip about 1½-inches wide, by about 2½-inches long. Cover half of the top of the cup with it, stretching it down at the sides and pasting it down all around.

Step 2. Cover the sides. Cut a strip of crepe paper across the grain ½-inch wider than your cups are deep. Gather a long strip of it on the sewing machine ¼-inch from one edge. Cut the strip into lengths sufficient to fit around the cups. Brush the outside of the cup lightly with paste. Place the gathered strip over the cup overlapping the ends about ½-inch and pasting them together.

Step 3. Make handle. From heavy note paper cut a strip for the handle. Brush paste on both sides and cover it with crepe paper. Paste the handle in place.

Step 4. Make spout. As the size of souffle cups vary, dimensions are not given. Cover a little square of note paper with crepe paper. Roll it into a tube. It's easy to do this over a pencil or knitting needle. Overlap and paste the ends together. Pinch one end and paste it down toward the bottom of the cup.

Step 5. Decorate the cup with ribbon and bow, tying the ribbon about ½-inch from the top of the cup. In Chapter IV you'll find complete directions for making perky, pretty bows. These bows add that distinctive professional touch to all party favors.

[60]

A Gum Drop Clothes Line—Place Mark

If it's a linen or "personal things" shower, mark the prospective bride's place at the luncheon table with a wee clothes line (*Fig. 32*). No name appears on the bride's place card; a place card for the other guests is also sketched in Figure 32.

It's as colorful as a rainbow. Two lemon yellow toothpicks are poked through two gumdrops, the lower one, green: the upper one, pink. The line is sky blue, the clothes and linens are wee patches of tissue paper in pretty pastel colors.

Fig. 32 Gum drop   Fig. 33 Tying clothes-
clothes line.   line and bow to toothpick.

Materials Needed to Make One Clothes Line:
Gum drops
Colored toothpicks
Crepe paper
Tissue paper
Paste
Colored crayons

Without directions you can copy this little place card for the bride, but here are some which will make it easier.

To make the clothes line, use light blue crepe paper as ribbon is too limp and too wide. Cut your strip ½-inch wide and make 20-inches of Crepe Paper Twist.[19] Cut it in two; then cut one of the halves in two. The shorter pieces are for the end bows; the longer for the line and end ties.

Tie the line to the poles: To do this easily, double one of the short pieces. Hold it in place against a toothpick, and tie it there near the top (*Fig. 33*), with one end of the 10-inch length. Tie the bow on the other toothpick in the same way. Snip the bow ends to different lengths, and perk out the loops with your fingers. To make the garments or

[61]

linens: Cut them with tiny scissors from tissue paper. Mark stripes, dots, etc. on the linens with colored pencils. Cut them double and fold them over the line. Cut the garments single, and paste them down.

PRETTY FROU-FROU FOR THE WEDDING BREAKFAST OR RECEPTION BUFFET

To MAKE A WEDDING PARTY the "prettiest ever"—fashion any or all of the seven decorations described below.

Bride and Groom Under an Arch

Of all wedding table centerpieces the most popular is this arch with wee dolls in bridal costumes (*Fig. 34*). This same decoration can be used for a Golden or Silver Wedding Anniversary. The bells hanging from the arch may be replaced with a gold "50" or a silver "25" cut from

Fig. 34 Wedding party centerpiece (approx. 15-inches high).

[62]

paper. Gold and silver paper can be used for the base, or "carpet" of the box.

The directions are for a centerpiece about 15-inches high.

Materials Needed to Make One Centerpiece:

1 box about 15 by 10 by 1½-inches
1 fold crepe paper white
1 fold crepe paper pale green
1 fold crepe paper light yellow
1 fold crepe paper flesh pink
1 fold crepe paper black
Scraps of red and blue paper
1 spool wire No. 1
8 wires No. 7 or 15
2 sheets silver wrapping paper
10 inches white lace or tulle
3 yards narrow satin ribbon
8 sprays artificial lilies of the valley
Paste, cotton, pliers or wire cutters

NOTE: *The scraps of red and blue paper are for the eyes and mouth of the dolls. These can be cut from colored ads.*

Step 1. Trim the box. Cover the box with silver wrapping paper. Paste a ruffle of white crepe paper around the sides of the box. Make the ruffle like this: Cut a strip [1] of crepe paper across the grain about ⅛-inch wider than the box is high. Gather it on the sewing machine along one edge leaving a narrow heading.

Step 2. Make the arches. These are wires wrapped, then bent; the center one stands about 13-inches high; the others about 10-inches. For each of the three arches use two No. 7 or 15 wires for thickness. For the center arch use the entire 36-inch length; for the two end arches, use 30-inches. Wrap [7] the wires with strips of white crepe paper ½-inch wide. Leave 3-inches on each end uncovered. Bend the wires to arch shape. Pierce holes in the box, push the unwrapped ends through. Bend the ends at right angles and fasten them down securely to the underside of the box with gummed tape.

Step 3. Make the center bell for the arch (*Fig. 35*). Cut a 4-inch square of white crepe paper. Fold and crease it across the grain through the middle. (If you have white Duplex crepe, you can use it by cutting a 2 by 4-piece with the grain running the 2-inch way.) Using the crease for the lower edge of the bell, overlap the short ends and paste them together, then gather the bell at the top with your fingers and tie it with a 6-inch piece of spool wire. Wrap the

See General Direction 1, *p.* 223; 7, *p.* 227

spool wire ends with a strip of white crepe ¼-inch wide. Place the lower edge of the bell on a flat surface and stretch it carefully to give a flared shape. Reach inside with your fingers and gently push the top out into bell shape. Tie the bell in place with the spool wire ends.

Step 4. Trim the arches. Make white satin bows and big maline or tulle bow, following the directions for tying bows on Page 106. Tuck a few sprays of artificial lilies-of-the-valley into them. Criss-cross satin ribbons around the arches, fastening the ends down with paste. Tie bows to the arch with the ends of the spool wire used for tying the bows.

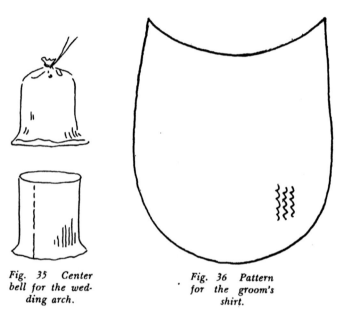

Fig. 35 Center bell for the wedding arch.

Fig. 36 Pattern for the groom's shirt.

Step 5. Make wire dolls for the bride and groom. Following the directions on Page 102 make your bride and groom two wire dolls standing about 8-inches high.

Step 6. Make the groom's trouser legs—two tubes of black crepe paper, pasted up "seam," and pasted to waist.

Step 7. Make his sleeves the same way, pasting on narrow cuffs first, if you wish.

Step 8. Cut and paste on a white shirt (*Fig. 36*). This shirt is a false front, no back to it. Paste it at the shoulders and around the edge.

It's stiffer made from Duplex crepe, but can be made from single.

Step 9. Cut and paste the vest *(Fig. 37)* at the shoulders and sides. Cut front opening, paste together and overlap the fronts.

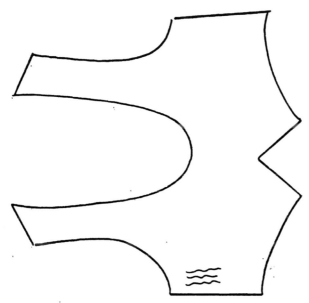

Fig. 37 Pattern for the groom's vest.

Step 10. Cut the coat *(Fig. 38)* from one piece of black crepe. Crease back the lapels. Put the coat on, pasting it down at the shoulders.

Step 11. Cut out from white writing paper a little collar. Paste it around the neck. Paste on a wee black tie.

Step 12. Make sleeves for the bride—two pieces of white crepe paper, pasted up seams, pasted around arms at shoulders, and tied with white satin bows at the wrists.

Step 13. Make the skirt of white crepe paper. Cut it the necessary length across the grain of the crepe. Gather it, making it very full. Paste it around her waist. Make a short overskirt in the same way.

Step 14. From white crepe paper, cut her bodice *(Figs. 39 and 40)* and paste it on at the shoulders and at the under-arm seams.

Step 15. Make two wide shoulder ruffles and paste them in place at neck line.

[65]

Step 16. Make a wide ruffle for her neck. Cut a strip of white paper across the grain about 1½-inches wide. Gather it leaving a heading. Paste it, along the gathers, around her neck.

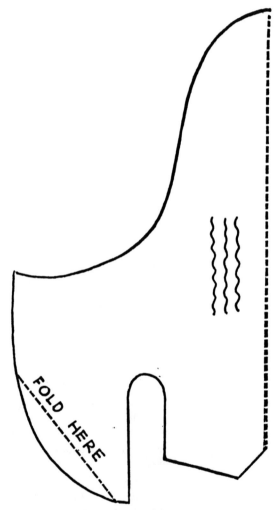

Fig. 38 Pattern for the groom's coat. Cut on fold.

Step 17. Paste on a maline, tulle, or lace veil.

Step 18. Bend her arms and tie a wee bouquet of flowers or a spray of artificial lilies-of-the-valley to them. Fasten both dolls to the box by tying their feet down with spool wire. Punch holes in the box first and thrust the wires through, twisting them together on the wrong side of the box.

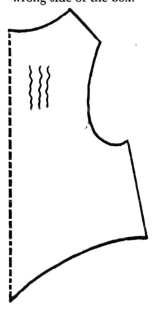
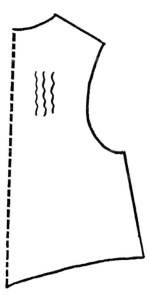

<table>
<tr><td>

Fig. 39 Pattern for the bride's bodice, front. Cut on fold.

</td><td>

Fig. 40 Pattern for the bride's bodice, back. Cut on fold.

</td></tr>
</table>

Wedding Bells to Hang in Arch

Many people like these *(Fig. 41)* to hang in the door-way between living room and dining room, or over an improvised altar in the home.

This bell is approximately 10-inches in diameter.

Materials Needed to Make One Bell:

1 wire No. 7

1 spool wire No. 1

1 fold crepe paper white

NOTE: *The No. 7 wire can be substituted by a wire ring 8 to 9-inches across.*

Step 1. Make a ring about 8- or 10-inches in diameter from your No. 7 wire, overlapping the ends at least 1½-inches. Fasten them with spool wire, then wrap the ring smoothly with a strip of white crepe cut ½-inch wide across the grain.

Step 2. Make the bell. From your fold of white crepe paper, cut off an 18-inch length. Fold, and crease it through the middle across the grain. This will give you a double strip 18-inches long, 10-inches wide.

Step 3. Place the wire ring inside the creased edge. Stretch the crepe paper around it carefully. Paste one of the doubled ends of crepe, inside the other, thus making a pasted seam.

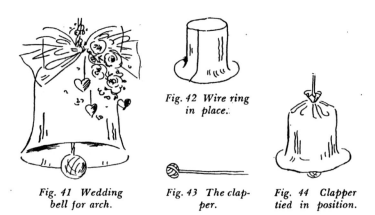

Fig. 41 Wedding bell for arch.

Fig. 42 Wire ring in place.

Fig. 43 The clapper.

Fig. 44 Clapper tied in position.

Step 4. Make the clapper (*Fig. 43*). Wad a piece of crepe paper into a ball. Tie a piece of white spool wire around it. Use the wire double and make it longer than the bell is deep. Wrap the ball and the spool wire with a strip of white crepe paper, cut about ½-inch across the grain. See Page 227 for wrapping with crepe paper.

Step 5. Put the clapper and bell together (*Fig. 44*). Gather the top of the bell with your fingers holding the clapper and its wire ends in place. Tie the top with spool wire (*Fig. 44*). Cut off any surplus crepe. Reach inside the bell and push out the top gently to shape it properly.

Step 6. Decorate the top with a big bow. See Page 106 for tying bows. A few sprays of artificial lilies-of-the-valley caught into it add a pretty touch.

Wedding Bell Nut Cup

A bell simply made of white crepe paper is placed like a cover over a paper souffle cup to form an attractive nut cup (*Fig. 45*) for the wedding breakfast. They are so attractive and pretty that they may be used as take-home favors. These nut cups carry out the bell theme used for room decoration.

Fig. 45 Wedding
bell nut cup.

Materials Needed to Make One Dozen:
>1 fold crepe paper white
>12 souffle cups
>1 spool wire white
>6 yards satin ribbon white, ½-inch wide
>6 sprays artificial lilies-of-the-valley
>Paste

NOTE: *Souffle cups are used as the forms or foundation cups. Those about 1¼-inch across are dainty for this wedding bell.*

Step 1. Cover the Foundation Cups. Across the grain of your white crepe paper, cut a strip ½-inch wider than the height of your cups. Brush the outside of the cup lightly with paste, then with the bottom edge of the strip even at the bottom of the cup stretch the strip around it. By stretching the paper tightly around the cup, the ½-inch extension will curl over the top edge. Paste the ends down neatly.

Step 2. Make Bell to Place over Cup. Across the grain of your white crepe, cut a strip 7-inches wide. For each cup, cut off a 6-inch length. Fold the strip in half across the grain. Overlap the 3½-inch ends

[69]

and seam them with paste. Gather the top with your fingers and tie it with white spool wire. Wrap [7] the surplus crepe at the top with a strip of white crepe cut about ½-inch wide. Place the lower edge of the bell on a table and stretch it to a flared shape. Put your fingers inside and push the top out into bell shape. Tie a satin bow to the top.

Heart Trimmed Cake Box

For the wedding cake this is a particularly attractive box (*Fig. 46*). Elaborate to look at, it is not difficult to make.

Fig. 46 (Left) Heart trimmed cake box (approx. 2½-inches high).

Fig. 47 (Right) Heart joined at tip.

Material Needed to Trim Twelve Boxes:

1 dozen wedding cake boxes
1 fold crepe paper white
3 wires No. 10
6 yards maline ribbon
Silver foil paper
Paste, gummed paper tape

NOTE: *Pink rose buds are optional for this.*
Cut a piece of No. 10 wire into four 9-inch lengths. Wrap [7] each one with a ¼-inch wide strip of white crepe paper. Starting with its center, leaving 1¼-inch ends at the tip, bend each wire into a heart shape. To make your hearts alike, it's a good idea to cut a pattern first, then shape each wire around the pattern. Join the heart at its tip by wrapping [7] the two wires for ¼-inch (*Fig. 47*). Punch a hole in the center top of each cake box. Put the two wire ends through it. Bend them at right angles and fasten them to the underside of the box lid with patches of gummed paper. Paste a sheet of silver paper on the inside of the box lid. Decorate the box with a maline bow into which you have thrust a tiny pink rose. For tying bows, see Page 106.

See General Direction 7, *p.* 227

Wedding Bell Place Card

This place card (*Fig. 48*) is very easy to make. On the end of a white card, paste two silver bells—cut from heavy silver wrapping paper—back to back, leaving the bottom part of the back bell loose so that you can perch the card over the edge of a tumbler. Silver wedding bells can be bought in many stationery stores in the form of gummed paper cut-outs.

*Fig. 48 Wedding
bell place card.*

Wedding Slipper Cake "Box"

This decorative cake "box" (*Fig. 49*) is an inexpensive way to present the small slices of take-home-and-dream-upon wedding cake to your guests. It's not a box, but simply two cut-outs in slipper shape of silver paper, tied with a fluffy maline bow and a few sprigs of lilies-of-the-valley (artificial), with the cake, waxed paper wrapped, sandwiched in between them.

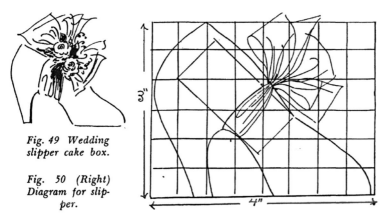

*Fig. 49 Wedding
slipper cake box.*

*Fig. 50 (Right)
Diagram for slip-
per.*

A pattern for making the slipper is shown in Figure 50. Enlarge it to the necessary size. A slipper 4-inches long by 3-inches high will conceal a piece of cake about 2¼-inches long and 1-inch high.

[71]

Cut slipper forms from lightweight cardboard. Brush paste over the cardboard and cover the forms with silver wrapping paper, cutting it to shape first. Be sure to cut half of your silver shapes facing in reverse.

Heart Shower Candle Holder

These candle holders *(Fig. 51)* are attractive for a buffet table placed against the wall. (Obviously, the candles can't be burned all the way down.)

To make them, you need for each candle, one cardboard heart covered with silver paper (about 3-inches from top to tip is a good size); about twenty small silver paper hearts. (You can probably buy these. Ask for "gummed paper hearts.") White satin ribbon, about 4⅓ yards for each candle. White spool wire.

Fig. 51 Heart shower candle holder.

Step 1. Make a shower of ribbons first. Cut six streamers for each candle, some short, some long enough to trail on the table. To the end of each paste two silver hearts back-to-back.

Step 2. Make bow with spool wire. Follow directions on Page 107.

Step 3. Tie cardboard heart to candle. Pierce two little holes in it, and with white spool wire tie the heart in place, letting the ends of the wire lie on top of the heart. The job will be complete after you cover the wire ends by pasting over them, first the six ribbon streamers, and last the bow itself.

WHAT TO MAKE FOR A STORK PARTY

YOU WANT SOMETHING attractive to hold the gifts. Nothing has ever surpassed the popularity of a giant bootee, daintily concocted of crepe paper and trimmed with ribbons, bows, and bits of paper lace. Just as popular, but more difficult to make is a Stork standing beside a chimney. The latter, of course, is laden with gifts.

The little nut cups sketched on Page 79 are easy to make, the Diaper taking the prize for simplicity as well as humor. The Bassinet is especially dainty, and very easy to make.

The Gift Holders may be used as centerpieces for the luncheon table or they may be placed on a little table which should be daintily draped with a white or pastel cover.

Baby Bootee Gift Holder

To hold little gift packages a bootee is easily whipped up from cardboard and crepe paper. The one described (*Fig. 52*) is about 14-inches long.

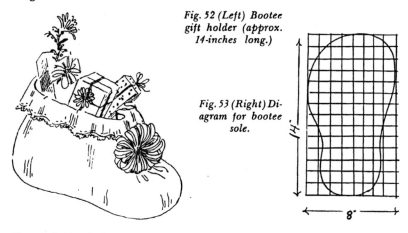

Fig. 52 (Left) Bootee gift holder (approx. 14-inches long.)

Fig. 53 (Right) Diagram for bootee sole.

8"

Materials Needed:
1 piece of heavy cardboard, 14 by 8-inches
1 fold crepe paper pale pink or blue
1 yard satin ribbon
2 yards approximately, narrow lace or paper lace edging
Paste

[73]

Step 1. Cut a cardboard sole enlarging the diagram given in Figure 53.

Step 2. Cut a strip [1] of pale pink crepe paper across the grain 12-inches wide, 40-inches long.

Step 3. Paste one long edge of the crepe paper to the bottom of the sole starting and ending at the center back. Use the paste sparingly. Cut off any surplus crepe. Overlap the two ends at the back and seam them with paste.

Step 4. At the top, turn down a cuff. Flute [3] the edges slightly. Sew lace, or paste paper lace edging, very lightly, to the bottom of the cuff.

Step 5. Make several little pleats at the center front. Catch them with a needle and thread.

Step 6. Make a satin bow, see page 106, and paste it in place. Last! Pile your prettily wrapped packages in the bootee.

Stork and Chimney Gift Holder

These directions are for a stork centerpiece (*Fig. 54*) that stands 16-inches high. A box about 7 to 8-inches high is a good proportion for the chimney.

Fig. 54 Stork and chimney gift holder (approx. 16-inches high).

See General Direction 1, *p.* 223; 3, *p.* 224

[74]

Materials Needed:

    2 pieces fairly heavy cardboard, 16 by 17-inches
    1 No. 7 or No. 15 wire
    1 No. 10 wire
    1 fold crepe paper white
    1 fold crepe paper black
    1 fold crepe paper orange
    1 box for chimney 7 to 8-inches high
    Red or pink wrapping paper to cover chimney
    White writing paper for top border of chimney
    Pen and black ink
    Tiny rubber doll
    Gummed paper tape, paste, wire cutters

Step 1. Make the chimney. Cover the box with red or pink wrapping paper. Mark it off into brick sections with white pastel crayon. Paste a border cut from white wrapping paper around the top.

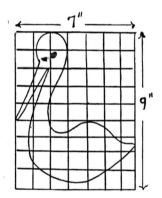

Fig. 55 The stork's foot.

Fig. 56 (Right) Diagram for stork's body.

Step 2. Make the stork's feet (*Fig. 55*). Cut six pieces of No. 10 wire, each about 3-inches long. Wrap each one with a strip of orange crepe paper cut across the grain about ¼-inch wide. Bend the wires to form toes of different lengths. See Page 227 for wrapping wires.

Step 3. Cut his legs. Cut two 10-inch lengths of No. 7 or 15 wire.

Step 4. Cut his body. Enlarge the diagram given in Figure 56. Cut two bodies from cardboard.

Step 5. Cut out the feathers. From black crepe paper, cut eight feathers; four for the tail, two for each wing, following pattern in Figure 57. Cut some white feathers using the same pattern. Cut others using the medium and small size patterns (*Figs. 58 and 59*). In cutting

[75]

these, follow the directions for cutting flower petals given on Page 229. The number needed varies with the degree they are over-lapped when pasted on.

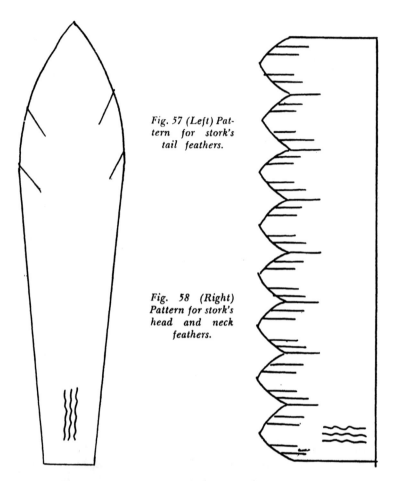

Fig. 57 (Left) Pattern for stork's tail feathers.

Fig. 58 (Right) Pattern for stork's head and neck feathers.

Step 6. Reinforce body of stork. Bend the piece of No. 7 or 15 wire left, after cutting off the two legs, to shape and with gummed paper patches fasten it down the center of the cardboard body *(Fig. 60)*.

Step 7. Complete the legs. Paste the wires forming the claws at the end of the wires forming the legs *(Fig. 61)*. Using a strip of orange crepe paper cut ½-inch wide across the grain, wrap the three toes securely to the legs.

Wrap[7] the legs for 8-inches. Wrap and rewrap them to make them thick and smooth.

Step 8. Gum tape the unwrapped parts of the legs to the cardboard body (*Fig. 60*).

Step 9. Paste the two cardboard bodies together.

Step 10. With strips of white crepe paper cut about 1-inch wide across the grain, wrap[7] the two bodies together. This is just to hold them together more securely and to cover the edges. It doesn't have to be done neatly.

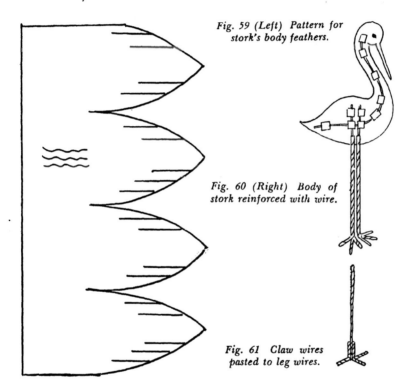

Fig. 59 (Left) Pattern for stork's body feathers.

Fig. 60 (Right) Body of stork reinforced with wire.

Fig. 61 Claw wires pasted to leg wires.

Step 11. Paste the feathers in place. Paste the black tail feathers on first, then working from tail to head cover the body with medium size white feathers, the head and neck with small ones. Work in rows placing the feathers of one row between the feathers of the previous row. In pasting, use the paste lightly on the flat end of the feathers only. Fluff feathers up a bit.

See **General Direction** 7, *p.* 227

[77]

Step 12. Cover the beak with orange crepe paper pasted in place. Cover the two edges first with narrow strips folded and placed over edge. Then cut out two pieces of orange crepe, beak size, and paste them on, front and back.

Step 13. Cut an oblong eye from white paper. Draw in a pupil and outline the eye with black ink. Paste it in place.

Step 14. Wrap a doll baby in a tiny handkerchief and fasten it to the end of the beak with pins or with bits of Scotch tape.

Step 15. Tie the stork to the side of the chimney. With a big pin, punch two holes near the top and two more just below the white border of the chimney. Tie the legs down with spool wire. This will look neat if you wrap the wire first with a narrow strip of orange crepe paper. Twist the wire ends together inside the box.

Fill the chimney with gifts for the baby, and the centerpiece is ready for the stork party.

Baby Carriage Nut Cup and Place Card

This little table decoration (*Fig. 62*) is so simple to make, even children can turn it out.

Fig. 62 Baby carriage nut cup and place card.

Materials Needed to Make Twelve Boxes:

12 small boxes
48 cardboard circles
           metal rim tags are fine if you can get them
2 No. 10 wires
1 sheet wrapping paper pink or blue
White paper lace edging
1 fold crepe paper white, pink or pale blue
12 place cards
4 yards satin ribbon
Paste

Step 1. Cut wire the desired length for handles. With a strip of crepe paper cut across the grain ¼-inch wide, wrap the handle. Bend handle and paste ends to outside of box.

Step 2. Cover box with wrapping paper, pink, blue, or white. Paste an edge of paper lace around the top.

Step 3. Paste wheels in place.

Step 4. Tie place card to carriage with satin ribbon and bow.

Diaper Nut Cup

One-two-three and this amusing nut cup (*Fig. 63*) is done.

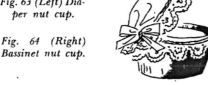

Fig. 63 (Left) Dia-
per nut cup.

Fig. 64 (Right)
Bassinet nut cup.

Materials Needed for One Dozen:

    12 nut cup foundations
    1 sheet tissue paper pink or white
    12 safety pins preferably gold
    Paste

Cut a triangular piece of tissue paper, place it around the nut cup and pin it in the center front. You may find it helpful to hold the diaper in place in the center back with a bit of paste.

Bassinet Nut Cup

Paper lace doilies and wee satin bows make this nut cup (*Fig. 64*) unusually dainty.

Materials Needed to Make One Dozen:

    12 foundation cups
    2 dozen small round paper lace doilies
    1 fold crepe paper pale pink or blue
    10 yards satin ribbon

Step 1. Cover the nut cup with pink or blue crepe paper. For Basic Method see Chapter IV.

Step 2. Paste a flounce of paper lace edging, cut from a doily, around the cup's edge.

Step 3. Make the bassinet hood. Slash a small round doily to its center. Overlap the two edges. Paste them down and paste the hood to the back of the nut cup.

Step 4. Tie satin bows, as shown in Chapter IV, and paste them to the sides.

THE GOLDEN WEDDING ANNIVERSARY

A PARTY HONORING the fiftieth anniversary rates particularly beautiful decorations. Something packed with sentiment, yet having dignity is required. Described below are three table centerpieces to choose from for this memorable occasion. Each is suitable for a luncheon, dinner party, or a buffet table at a reception.

Bride-and-Groom Under the Arch Centerpiece

One of the most popular table decorations is the bride-and-groom under an arch shown on Page 62. By covering the base with a sheet of gold wrapping paper, dressing the little figures in old-fashioned costumes, and by hanging from the center arch, the number "50," cut from gold paper, you have one of the best-loved Golden Wedding Centerpieces.

The Aisle of Life Centerpiece

Another Golden Wedding Centerpiece (*Fig. 65*) using the little dolls dressed in old-fashioned bridal costumes carries out the idea of

Fig. 65 Golden Wedding table centerpiece. The dolls are approximately 8-inches tall.

Marching Up the Aisle of Life Together. The bride and groom are toward one end of the table; toward the other is an "altar" of six candles. Stretching between them is a gold carpet. This is a long piece of gold paper across which, at intervals, are lines marking (with captions) "Fifth Anniversary," "Twenty-fifth Anniversary," and so on, up to fifty. Gardenias, or other flowers can edge the golden aisle.

Golden Wreath Centerpiece

Golden leaves framing the important numerals "50" is the time honored favorite for Golden Wedding Celebrations, also the easiest of all the anniversary centerpieces to make. See Figure 66.

THE SILVER WEDDING ANNIVERSARY

DECORATIONS FOR A PARTY celebrating the twenty-fifth anniversary often dramatize the numerals "25." Covered with silver the numerals can be used in various ways. The table centerpieces shown in this book for the Golden Anniversary are also suitable for the Silver Anniversary when silver papers are substituted for gold.

Fig. 66 Silver Wedding table centerpiece (approx. 12-inches high).

Silver Wreath Centerpiece

Traditional favorite for a party celebrating the twenty-fifth anniversary is this centerpiece bearing the numerals "25" (*Fig. 66*). Leaves, numerals, and box-base are of silver paper; the bow is white maline; the ruffle, clear transparent cellophane.

[81]

Materials Needed for One Centerpiece:

2 No. 7 or 15 wires
1 spool No. 1 wire
10 ready-made silver leaf sprays or silver foil paper to make leaves
1 fold crepe paper for wrapping wires, white
Cardboard for numerals
6 yards maline ribbon
1 shallow box 10 to 12-inches square
1 roll clear transparent cellophane
1 piece narrow silver ribbon, about 1⅓ yards
Silver foil paper to cover the box
Gummed paper tape, paste, pliers or wire cutters

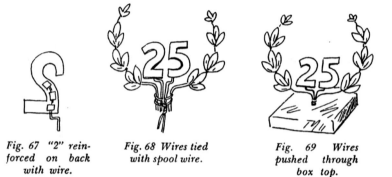

Fig. 67 "2" rein-
forced on back
with wire.

Fig. 68 Wires tied
with spool wire.

Fig. 69 Wires
pushed through
box top.

Step 1. Wrap [7] two No. 7, 24-inch wires with a strip of white crepe paper ½-inch wide.

Step 2. Fasten silver leaves to all but 4-inches at the end of each wire. Fasten them by wrapping the leaves' stems to the 20-inch stems. Use white crepe paper for the wrapping. Bend wires to shape. If you are making your own leaves, use any small leaf in Chapter I. Cut the leaves from silver foil paper and paste a No. 10 wire down the center back of each allowing about 2-inches of the wire to extend below the leaf.

Step 3. Make numerals (*Fig. 67*). Cut the 25 from cardboard. Attach a 9-inch length of No. 7 or 15 wire to the back of each number with patches of gummed paper tape. Cover the numbers, front and back, with silver foil paper. If the foil is light weight, cover the back of the numerals neatly with duplicate numerals before pasting on the foil.

Step 4. Tie all the wires together with spool wires (*Fig. 68*). Wrap them together for one inch with a strip of white crepe paper ½-inch wide.

Step 5. Cover the box top with metallic paper pasting it only on the inside of the box where it is turned under.

Step 6. Push the wires through a hole in the center of the box (*Fig. 69*). On the underside spread them out and fasten them down with gummed paper tape.

Step 7. Tie two maline bows to the base. See Page 106 for making bows.

Step 8. Make a ruffle 2½-inches wide of tarletan, white crepe paper,[15] or clear transparent cellophane for the base. Paste it in place. Here's a trick for handling a cellophane ruffle. Before ruffling it, stitch to one long edge a ½-inch wide strip of crepe paper. Gather the crepe paper and paste it to the cardboard foundation. Paste won't hold cellophane, but it will crepe paper.

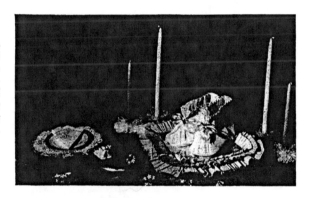

For a stork party, two bootees make a sentimental centerpiece. The two photographed are small editions of the bootee for which directions are given on Page 73.

This bride has "bones" of wire and "flesh" of crepe paper, easy to make according to the directions for making Novelty Dolls on Page 102.

See General Direction 15, *p.* 231

[83]

CHAPTER III

How to Make Decorations and Favors for Year-Round Happenings

A CIRCUS BIRTHDAY PARTY FOR CHILDREN

A BIRTHDAY PARTY table decked out like a three-ring circus is a sure-fire way to a child's heart, or, for that matter, to anyone's heart.

A Three-Ring Centerpiece

This table decoration (*Fig. 1*) requires no finger acrobatics to make. One, only, of the rings is sketched. In the other two, made in exactly the same way, the clown acrobats can perform equally hair-raising stunts.

Fig. 1 *Circus party table center-piece (approx. 18-inches high).*

Materials Needed to Make One Ring:
    5 wires No. 7 or 15
    1 spool wire No. 1 or 2
    1 fold crepe paper white

[84]

1 fold crepe paper red
2 folds crepe paper yellow
2 pieces cardboard 16 by 12-inches
Scraps of black, red and bright blue paper
Paste, gummed paper tape

NOTE: *The black, red and bright blue paper are for the clown's features and may be cut from colored advertisements.*

Step 1. Following the directions in Chapter IV, make a clown doll, using two No. 7 or 15 wires—12-inches long—for the arms, body and legs. Use white crepe paper for the head and body. Paste on features cut from colored paper.

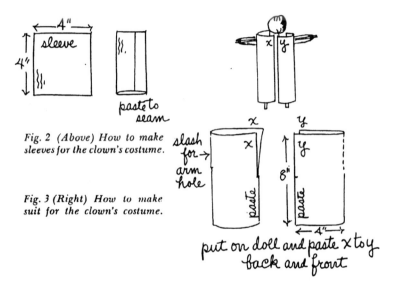

Fig. 2 (*Above*) *How to make sleeves for the clown's costume.*

Fig. 3 (*Right*) *How to make suit for the clown's costume.*

Step 2. Dress the clown. Cut the sleeves from yellow crepe paper (*Fig. 2*). Gather them with your fingers and paste them at the shoulders and wrists. Cut the suit from yellow crepe (*Fig. 3*). Paste it down around the neck and ankles. Make ruffs: Cut strips [1] of red and white crepe paper across the grain, 2½-inches wide for the neck; 1½-inches for the wrists and ankles. Gather them on a sewing machine through the center length. Cut them to the necessary length. Tie them around neck, wrists and ankles with spool wire.[6] Cut a circle about 5-inches in diameter, of note paper—for a cone hat. Cut it in two. Cover the semi-circle with bright crepe or other paper. Overlap

See General Direction 1, *p.* 223; 6, *p.* 226

[85]

and seam the two straight edges with paste. Paste it on.

Step 3. Make the uprights and trapeze. Make each of the two uprights with three (for thickness) No. 7 or 15 wires, 18-inches long. Wrap [7] them together with strips of yellow crepe paper cut ½-inch wide across the grain. Leave a 1½-inch length of the three wires unwrapped at one end. Make the crossbar of one piece of No. 15 wire. Wrap it in the same way. Tie it to the uprights with spool wire. Make trapeze of No. 7 wires, wrapping them with red crepe and tying them together and to the crossbar with spool wire.

Step 4. Make the base, or ring. Cut two oval pieces of cardboard, approximately 16 by 12-inches. Punch holes in one for the uprights. Push unwrapped wires through the holes. Spread the wires out chicken-foot fashion on the underside of the cardboard. Fasten them down with bits of gummed paper. Paste the two ovals together.

Step 5. Trim the ring. Cover the top with yellow crepe paper crushed.[16] Make ruffles for the edge. Cut one strip [1] from red crepe paper, another from yellow crepe; one about 6-inches wide across the grain of the crepe, the other about 4-inches. If you have pinking shears, use them to make an attractive edge. Gather them down the center length and paste them around the ring, the smaller one inside the larger. Use paste sparingly along the gathers.

Clown Bag of Peanuts

"Something to take home" so necessary to the success of a child's party is provided by this Clown Bag of Peanuts (*Fig. 4*).

Fig. 4 Clown bag of pea-
nuts (approx. 4-inches
high).

Fig. 5 Pattern for clown's
head.

See General Direction 7, *p.* 227; 16, *p.* 232; 1, *p.* 223

Materials Needed for One Dozen:

> 1 fold crepe paper (one or two colors for each bag)
> 1 spool wire No. 1 or 2
> White construction paper or lightweight cardboard
> Crayons—black, red and blue

Step 1. Cut clown's heads and hats, two for each bag, from white construction paper. See Pattern (*Fig. 5*). Color the features on one with crayons. Paste the two heads together with a toothpick extending between them to form a long neck.

Step 2. Tie the peanuts in a 14-inch square of crepe paper, inserting the toothpick neck in the bag. A paper napkin can be used in place of the paper. Trim the uneven edges of the square, and tie a ruff around the clown's neck. Make it as described in Step 2. under "A Three Ring Centerpiece."

Lollipop Clown

Another "take home" favor for a child's party, this Lollipop Clown (*Fig. 6*) is easy to make.

Fig. 6 Lollipop clown.

Fig. 7 Tent candy cup.

Materials Needed to Make Lollipop Clowns:

> Lollipops
> Crepe paper, any circus color
> Cardboard, lightweight
> Crayons, black, red and blue
> Paste

[87]

Wrap a strip of crepe paper around the lollipop.[7] Using Figure 5 as a guide, cut out the clown's head and hat from white cardboard. Color it with crayons and paste it over the lollipop. Make a ruff as described in Step 2. under "A Three Ring Centerpiece." Tie it in place.

Tent Candy Cup

A parade of Tent Candy Cups (*Fig. 7*) around the birthday table, will say as plainly as words, "Here's a circus!"

Materials Required to Make One Dozen:
    12 foundation nut cups
    1 fold crepe paper yellow
    1 fold crepe paper red
    1 fold crepe paper white
    Toothpicks
    Paste

Step 1. Cover the nut cups with yellow crepe paper. See Chapter IV, Basic Method.

Step 2. Cut a circle large enough for the "big top" from note paper. Cover it with another circle cut from yellow crepe paper. Apply the paste lightly to the note paper. Slash the circle to the center in one place. Overlap the two edges and paste them together to form the tent top. Across the grain of the yellow crepe, cut a strip ½-inch wide.[1] Stretch and paste it around the edge to form a wee "awning." Cover the upper edge of the yellow "awning" with a very narrow strip of red crepe cut across the grain. Brush the paste very lightly on the cup's edge and stretch the red strip as you lay it in place. Cut a small red paper pennant. Paste it to a toothpick. Stick the toothpick in place and the cup is complete.

A SWEETHEART BIRTHDAY PARTY FOR GIRLS

IF SHE'S PASSED the Mother Goose stage, a Sweetheart Party will delight her. The centerpiece described below can also be used for Valentine Parties and Brides' Showers.

A Heart Full of Gifts Centerpiece

This sentimentally be-frilled heart (*Fig. 8*) sits on a box filled with tiny gifts which are tied to ribbons ending at each guest's place. At a given signal the little girls pull the ribbons and out pop presents for each.

Materials Needed to Make One Centerpiece:
    2 wires No. 7
    1 spool wire No. 2

See General Direction 7, *p.* 227; 1, *p.* 223

1 fold crepe paper pink
1 sheet tissue paper pink
1 package paper lace doilies white
10 yards satin ribbon pink
1 box, about 10-inches square and 2-inches deep

Fig. 8 *Heart full of gifts center-piece (approx. 15-inches high.)*

Fig. 9 Wires wrapped, bent and tied to form heart shape.

Step 1. Make the heart. With white crepe paper, cut in a strip ½-inch wide,[1] wrap[7] two lengths of No. 7 wire put together to obtain a 45-inch length. Bend them to a heart shape and tie them together 6-inches from the ends with spool wire, for two inches (*Fig. 9*).

Step 2. Decorate the heart. Cut a strip[1] of pink crepe paper 8-inches wide. Gather it down the center length to form a double ruffle. Paste it over the wire heart, applying the paste lightly to the heart. Cut lace edgings from round paper doilies and paste them in place. Add several bows, tiny artificial flowers, and loops of ribbon, pasting them all in position. For tying bows, see Chapter IV.

Step 3. Decorate the base. Cut a strip[1] of pink crepe paper a trifle wider than the box is high. Gather it down the center length to form a double and very full ruffle. Paste it, along its gathers, around the box. Apply the paste to the box, not to the ruffle.

Step 4. Fasten the heart to the box by spreading the wires out and fastening them down to the inside bottom of the box with gummed paper tape.

See General Direction 1, *p.* 223; 7, *p.* 227

Step 5. Place the presents with their long ribbon streamers inside the box. Cover the top with some strips of pink tissue paper laid on lattice fashion, pasting the ends to the sides of the box. Bring the ends of the gift ribbons out through the openings in the lattice work and place one at each guest's place with a place card tied to it.

Step 6. Place a paper doily around the base of the heart, and the project is complete.

WHAT TO MAKE FOR HOLIDAY PARTIES

BOTH CHILDREN AND ADULTS like to celebrate the holidays with something special. The centerpieces described in this section will make any gathering merrier, whether it be for home, office, school, church or a special social gathering.

A Grab Bag Santa Claus

The Santa sketched (*Fig. 10*) is roundly fat because he's full of gifts. Make him one year and use him every year as long as there's fun in your heart. He stands about 30-inches high and holds only smallish gifts.

Fig. 10 Grab bag Santa Claus (approx. 30-inches high).

Materials Needed to Make One Centerpiece:
  2 folds crepe paper red
  1 fold crepe paper pink
  1 round hat box (or paper tub) 12-inches in diameter and 7-inches high
  1 box cotton
  ½-yard glazed paper black for belt
  3 wires No. 7 or 15

[90]

1 spool wire No. 1 or 2
3 yards ribbon red, ½-inch wide
Scraps of bright blue paper for eyes
Paste, wire cutters or pliers

Step 1. Make the bag (*Fig. 11*). Use a whole fold of red crepe. Gather it along the entire 10-feet and paste it to the bottom of the round box, 1-inch from the edge. With coarse thread gather the crepe loosely 4-inches from the top.

Step 2. Make a 5-inch wide ruffle of red crepe,[15] and paste it around the bottom of the box, on top of the other crepe.

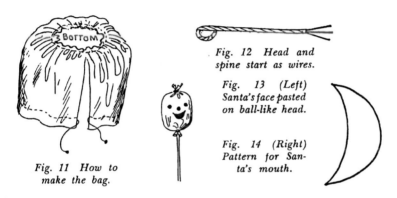

Fig. 11 How to make the bag.

Fig. 12 Head and spine start as wires.

Fig. 13 (Left) Santa's face pasted on ball-like head.

Fig. 14 (Right) Pattern for Santa's mouth.

Step 3. Make Santa's head and spine (*Fig. 12*). Wrap [7] three No. 7 or 15 wires, 30-inches long, together with a ½-inch wide strip of flesh pink crepe. Stop 5-inches short of one end. At the other end, bend the wires 3-inches down to form a loop. Wrap cotton around the loop to make the stuffing for the head. Then wrap the loop with a strip of pink crepe paper cut about 1-inch wide until the head is 4-inches thick.

Step 4. Make Santa's face (*Fig. 13*). Cut a 15-inch square of flesh pink crepe. Stretch it slightly. Wrap it around the head with the grain of the crepe running from skull to chin. Overlap the two ends and join them with paste. Tie the crepe together at the top, then under the chin with spool wire.[6] Cut off any surplus crepe at the top. Paste on the features. Cut circles of blue for the eyes, a half moon of red for the mouth (*Fig. 14*), and cover a cotton ball with a stretched square of red crepe paper for the nose. Paste the crepe paper down to the back of the ball, then paste the nose in position. Cut the eyebrows, beard and mustaches from cotton and paste them in place.

See General Direction 7, *p.* 227; 15, *p.* 231; 6, *p.* 226

Step 5. Put Santa in the bag. Spread the uncovered parts of the wires out chicken-foot fashion and fasten them with gummed tape to the inside bottom of the bag. Santa's bag suit should open down the front. Remember that when you put him in the bag. Now draw the gathering threads at the top of the bag tightly and tie them around the old man's neck.

Step 6. Paste on a shiny paper belt and buttons. Make a cap by cutting a strip of red crepe 12-inches wide, 15-inches long. Paste or stitch the two 12-inch sides together. Turn up a 1-inch brim at the bottom. Paste the hat on, turn the top down, tie it, and paste a white cotton pompon in place. A sprig of holly or two completes Santa's costume.

St. Patrick's Day Balloon Faces

These balloon faces (*Fig. 15*) are hilarious fun, and fun to make. Molly and Mike centering the supper table will add punch to any Wearin' of the Green Party. Balloon faces like these can be used for all sorts of parties. It's easy to make Santa Claus and Clowns, for example.

Fig. 15 *Balloon centerpieces for
a St. Patrick's day party table.*

Materials Needed to Make Two Faces:
>2 balloons white
>1 fold crepe paper white
>1 fold crepe paper green
>1 fold crepe paper black
>1 fold crepe paper red
>Green cardboard for Mike's hat
>2 men's white stiff collars

[92]

Tempera paints, colors blue, red, white
Scotch tape

Step 1. Blow up the two balloons and fasten them in place on the men's collars with short lengths of Scotch tape. Put the tape strips on the "wrong" side, half on the collars, half on the balloons.

Step 2. Make hair. For Molly's, cut a strip of black crepe paper, 3-inches wide.[1] Slash it into a coarse, wide fringe.[2] Curl the ends over a scissors blade.[5] Fasten curls around Molly's face with short strips of Scotch tape. Make Mike's red curls and sideburns in the same way.

Step 3. Dress Molly and Mike in green. Tie a green crepe paper bow and fasten it with Scotch tape to Mike's collar. See Chapter IV for making bows. Tie a white crepe paper kerchief around Molly's neck and a green one around her head. It is best to stretch the crepe paper slightly. To make Mike's hat, cut a green cardboard circle 14-inches in diameter. From the center of it, cut a 6-inch circle. Cut the crown 8-inches high and 20-inches long. Paste the 8-inch sides together. Hold it to the brim with short lengths of Scotch tape or tie on a white headband.

Step 4. Paint on the features. Mix Tempera paints with a little soap and give Molly and Mike blue eyes, rosy cheeks and red lips.

Turkey Gobblers for Thanksgiving

Several little turkeys (*Fig. 16*) flanking a pumpkin holding fruits, will add spice to any Thanksgiving table.

Materials Needed to Make Three Turkey Gobblers:

1 fold crepe paper brown
1 fold crepe paper light green
1 fold crepe paper red
2 wires No. 9 or 10
Scotch tape, knitting needle, scrap of cardboard

Step 1. Make the body (this is a pompon). Cut a strip of brown crepe paper 2½-inches wide and 25-inches long.[1] Fold the strip in two along the 25-inch length. Cut the unfolded edges into fine slashes, to within ¼-inch of the fold. Gather the strip through the center over a knitting needle.[15] Slip an 8-inch length of No. 9 wire under the gathers and tie it very tightly. Twist, don't knot the wires. Fluff the fringe up to make a pompon.

Step 2. Make the tail. Cut a strip [1] of red, green and brown crepe 8-inches long, and in these widths: red, 5-inches; green, 4¾-inches; brown, 4½-inches. Fold each piece in two, down the 8-inch length and cut

See General Direction 1, *p.* 223; 2, *p.* 223; 5, *p.* 225; 15, *p.* 231

the unfolded edges into ½-inch wide scallops. Open the strips up. Put the green over the red, and the brown over the green. Fold them again down the center length with the brown on the outside, and gather them over a knitting needle. Slip an 8-inch length of No. 9 wire under the gathers and tie the strips firmly through the center. With your fingers, spread the scallops out into a fan shape. Take one of the body wires and one of the tail wires and wrap them together [7] with a ½-inch wide strip of orange crepe, thus forming a leg. Form the other leg in the same way. Bend each wire to form a foot.

Fig. 16 Turkey gobblers for the Thanksgiving table (approx. 4-inches high).

Step 3. Make the neck and head. Cut a 4-inch square of brown crepe paper. Wrap it tightly around a knitting needle, thus forming a cylinder with the grain of the crepe running up and down. Paste down the loose end lightly. Crush the crepe by pushing it with your fingers from each end toward the center. Push hard. Remove the needle. Stretch the crushed crepe out slightly to form a crinkly neck. At one end, pinch the cylinder to close it. To that end, paste a bit of red crepe for a beak and a small triangle of red for the wattle.

Step 4. With Scotch tape fasten the turkey's feet to a piece of cardboard cut in leaf shape. The turkey is now ready for the table.

Halloween Witchery

Skeletons dancing on the brim of a witch's hat (*Fig. 17*) makes a centerpiece for the Halloween refreshment table. No black magic is required to make it.

See General Direction 7, *p.* 227

Materials Needed to Make One Centerpiece:
   1 fold crepe paper white
   Black shiny cardboard
   Chenille pipe cleaners
   Cotton
   Black India Ink
   Scraps of silver and gold foil paper

*Fig. 17   Witch's hat for a
Halloween party table.*

Step 1. Make the hat. Cut a 14-inch circle for the hat's brim. To cut the peaked crown, make a pattern by cutting a 34-inch circle from wrapping paper. Cut the circle in two and roll it to a cone shape. When you have the size crown you want, trim the wrapping paper, then cut the black paper. Fasten the sides together with paste. Place it on the brim. Paste on nocturnal decorations, such as stars and moon, cut from the foil paper.

Step 2. Make the skeletons. For the heads, wind balls of cotton with narrow strips of white crepe paper.[1] Draw the features with pen and black India Ink. Leave a little neck of cotton and paper to wind in with the backbone. Make the bone and legs of two pipe cleaners. The extra strength of two cleaners is needed to hold up the heads. Make each arm of one cleaner. Twist the cleaners to spiral shape. As they are easy to handle, no lesson in anatomy is necessary for putting them together. Arms and legs can be joined to the body simply by clamping the end of one cleaner around another. Fasten the dancers to the hat's brim with patches of Scotch tape.

See General Direction 1, *p.* 223

[95]

A Stars and Stripes Centerpiece

Simplest of all centerpieces, yet effective, is this box bursting with red, white and blue frou-frou (*Fig. 18*). Crepe paper or cellophane can make the bouffant center.

By changing the color scheme and the cut-out decorations on the outside of the box, this type centerpiece can be made suitable for any of the seasonal holidays. For Easter, fill it with yellow, green and purple ruffles and paste a bunny cut-out to the outside; for Halloween, fill it with yellow and black ruffles and paste a witch on her broom to the outside; for Valentine's Day, make the ruffles of pink, red and white and decorate the outside with paper lace doilies and cut-outs of hearts and cupid.

Fig. 18 (Left) Stars and stripes centerpieces (approx. 14-inches high).

Fig. 19 (Above) Three ruffles tied together.

Materials Needed to Make One Box:
    1 fold crepe paper or cellophane red
    1 fold crepe paper or cellophane white
    1 fold crepe paper or cellophane blue
    1 box 6-inches high and 7-inches square
    Silver stars, spool wire

NOTE: *The silver stars may be bought as gummed seals.*

No steps are necessary for this simple project. Cut three strips[1] of crepe paper about 10 to 14-inches wide. Open them up and gather each along one edge with your fingers, into a ruffle. Tie each ruffle (*Fig. 19*) separately with string, picture wire or spool wire, then tie all together. If you're using cellophane, gather it on the machine just as you would cloth or crepe paper.

See General Direction 1, *p.* 223

Centerpieces for Around the Calender

Using the ideas illustrated in Figures 20, 21 and 22, you can whip up a decoration for practically any occasion in record time. You need only a No. 7 or 15 wire, two paper or cardboard cut-outs and a little ribbon. For a little favor, use a No. 10 wire; for a big table centerpiece, a No. 7 or No. 15 wire. See the wire chart in Chapter XV.

Fig. 20 Hallo- ween party table favor or center- piece.   *Fig. 21 Christmas party table favor or centerpiece.*   *Fig. 22 Valen- tine's Day party table favor or cen- terpiece.*

For St. Valentine's, use heart cut-outs; for St. Patrick's, shamrocks; for Halloween, a witch. School initials, club and church symbols, birthday or anniversary numerals 25—50 (cut from gold or silver foil), can also be used. Carry out the seasonal or club colors in the wrapping of the wire and in the bow or other decorations.

Step 1. Wrap the wire with crepe paper [7] and bend the wire to a circular base.

Step 2. Paste two cut-outs at the top with the wire sandwiched between them. Remember, in making cut-outs that one must be in reverse.

Step 3. Decorate the wire base with bows, flowers or foliage.

FUN WITH FAVORS

THE CHERRY ON the sundae! Favors add that final zip of color and gaiety to a party. Grown-ups in grown-up (non-party) mood can skip them, but for children the little "take-home" favors add the thrill that lingers.

The gaieties illustrated and described on the following pages are so simple that no step-by-step directions are necessary. To look at the sketches is to see, practically, how they are made.

See General Direction 7, p. 227

[97]

Marshmallow Snowman

This fellow (*Fig. 23*) is two marshmallows and one gumdrop with raisin features stuck on a tooth pick. His hat is black crepe paper; his scarf, red cellophane. (Twist the ends together. They'll hold together. If they have a tendency to fly apart, a little water will hold them.)

Lollipop Santa Claus

His face (*Fig. 24*) is a ready-made gummed paper seal; his hair and beard are cotton; his cap and the winding on the lollipop stick are red crepe paper. Tinsel ribbon is bright for the bow.

Fig. 23 Marsh-
mallow snowman.

Fig. 24 Lollipop
Santa Claus.

Fig. 25 Red mit-
ten candy bags.

Red Mitten Candy Bags

Kitten size, each bag (*Fig. 25*) will hold a few nuts and candies. Stitch them up from red calico or two thicknesses (front and back) of red crepe paper. If you can get Duplex crepe, a single thickness is strong enough. Paste or sew on the ribbons.

Lollipop Sweetheart

Here's a cardboard heart (*Fig. 26*) covered with ruffles of pink crepe paper pasted on. The lollipop and its stick are wrapped with a strip of pink crepe paper. The cardboard heart and its silver bows are pasted on.

Jingle Bell Clown

Shake him (*Fig. 27*) and his bells ring; undress him, and there's a pencil. His head is crepe paper. The fringe to which the bells are sewed is straight crepe paper fringe, red and yellow. His hat and bow are yellow crepe paper.

Marshmallow Clown

His features (*Fig. 28*) are raisins. He rests on a turquoise crepe paper ruffle which has been pasted to a paper lace doily. His cone-shaped hat is cerise crepe paper, a semi-circle folded and pasted to shape.

Fig. 26 Lollipop sweetheart.

Fig. 27 Jingle bell clown.

Fig. 28 Marshma'low clown.

Scarecrow Jack

His body (*Fig. 29*) which is full of nuts is a round orange crepe paper bag; his jiggly arms and neck are corkscrew spool wires; his head and arms are paper cut-outs; his hat is crepe paper.

Fig. 29 Scarecrow Jack bag of nuts.

Fig. 30 A daisy return ball.

Fig. 31 Chewing gum pup tent.

Return Ball—a Daisy

Each child at the party must have one (*Fig. 30*). The ball fits into a paper nut (soufflé) cup which forms the bonnet. A strip of yellow crepe paper daisy petals is pasted around the cup's edge. Paper eyes and mouth are pasted on.

Chewing Gum Pup Tent

This tent (*Fig. 31*) is quick-as-a-wink to make! Wrap a stick of gum in manila wrapping paper. Bend it. Poke a hole in the center. Insert a tooth pick. (A colored one is gay.) Paste a colored paper flag, bearing place card initials, to the pole.

Fig. 32 Chewing gum soldier.	*Fig. 33 Peppermint stick sailboat.*	*Fig. 34 Indian tent birthday cake.*

Chewing Gum Soldier

Here is a package of chewing gum (*Fig. 32*) wrapped in red paper, neatly pasted at strategic points. A white band of paper on which features are inked, forms the toy soldier's face; silver passe-partout (it is gummed on one side) forms the shining trappings.

Peppermint Stick Sailboat

Its mast (*Fig. 33*) is made of two toothpicks wrapped together with a narrow strip of blue crepe paper.[1] The pale green sail is crepe paper. The bow which ties the mast to the candy boat is blue crepe paper twist.[19]

Indian Tent Birthday Cake

The tent (*Fig. 34*) is a semi-circle of brown wrapping paper closed with paste and decorated with paper cut-out moon, stars and sun. At given signals each guest in turn may remove the tent, light the candle, make a wish and blow the candle out. Good luck guaranteed!

See General Direction 1, *p.* 223; 19, *p.* 233

Graduation Diploma and Mortarboard

The paper napkin and ribbon carry out the school colors. In the diploma (*Fig. 35*) is written a fortune; on it is a name, so that it serves as a place card. The Mortarboard is simply a square of black cardboard.

Fig. 35 Graduation diploma and mortarboard.

Fig. 36 Uncle Sam's hat.

Uncle Sam's Hat

Good for The Fourth, February 12 or 22nd, or other Patriotic holidays. The hat (*Fig. 36*) is a paper drinking cup striped with red, gummed paper tape. The blue hat band has silver gummed stars on it. The circular brim is two layers of blue crepe paper pasted together.[10] The brim's sides are curled over a pencil. Candies or cigarettes are wrapped in a square of clear transparent cellophane which flares out.

Favors make the party, as illustrated by this attractive table setting.

See General Direction 10, *p.* 228

CHAPTER IV

Making Novelty Dolls, Tying Bows and Decorating Nut Cups

HOW TO MAKE NOVELTY DOLLS

NOVELTY DOLLS WITH simply made wire bodies are used for many purposes: for party decorations (*Fig. 1*), for dressing-table decorations (*Fig. 2*), for bed pillow novelties, for school-room projects (*Fig. 3*), for fashion studies. As little as 2-inches, or as big as twenty, they are made in this

Fig. 1 Clown doll as a party decoration.	*Fig. 2 Novelty doll for dressing table.*	*Fig. 3 Dolls for a school project.*

basic way. *First.* Make the head (*Fig. 4*). *Second.* Wrap [1] wires with crepe paper, then bend them to form legs and body (*Fig. 5*). *Third.* Tie legs and body and head together (*Fig. 6*). *Fourth.* Wrap wires [7] to form arms (*Fig. 7*). *Fifth.* Wrap arms to body. Bend them to position (*Fig. 8*). *Sixth.* Add hair and features to head (*Fig. 8*).

Now for details. Use No. 10 or 9 wires for dolls under 2-inches, No. 7 for up to 6-inches, No. 7 or 15 wires for larger dolls. See Wire Chart in Chapter XV. The measurements for the arms, legs-and-body are all the same length; the head is a little less than one-fourth the complete height.

Step 1. Make the head. You can use any sort of head: china, cloth, cardboard circle, or crepe paper. The latter, widely used, is made like this:

Make its shape. Cut a square of crepe paper twice the finished head

See General Direction 1, *p.* 223; 7, *p.* 227

length. With the grain of the crepe running from top to bottom
overlap and paste the ends together (*Fig. 9*). Stuff the tube thus
formed with cotton to head size. Tie the top with spool wire. To
use the spool wire, cut off a sufficient length—say 8-inches. Double

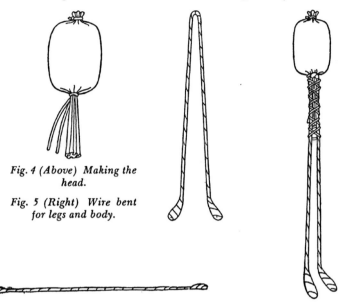

*Fig. 4 (Above) Making the
head.*

*Fig. 5 (Right) Wire bent
for legs and body.*

Fig. 7 Wire wrapped to form arms.

*Fig. 6 Legs, body
and head tied to-
gether.*

it like a hair pin. Place the top in the hairpin curve, then twist the
ends together tightly. Cut off any surplus. Tie the neck with spool
wire (*Fig. 4*). Don't cut the surplus crepe off at "neck."

Add the features. Note Figures 10 and 11. In Figure 10 the features are
cut out and pasted on; in Figure 11 they are drawn in with a fine
pen and black India Ink. They are given color with pastel crayons.
The cheeks are rouged.

Add the hair. Curly hair: make narrow strips of curly fringe,[20] then,
starting at the hair line, paste them around and around in overlapping rows till you reach the top of the skull. Straight hair: make
it in the same way with straight fringe.[2] A little wig (*Fig. 12*) can
also be made by cutting pieces of crepe paper to fit the skull. Slash
the edges into fringe with the grain and curl them [5] over a scissors
blade. Paste them in place cutting them to necessary length. See

See General Direction 20, *p.* 234; 2, *p.* 223; 5, *p.* 225

"Wigs," Chapter VI. For very tiny dolls, hair can be drawn on with pastel crayons. A bow or hat can cover the spool wire tie at the top of the head. White cotton can be pasted on for Colonial Doll wigs. Corkscrew curls can be made from long narrow strips [1] of crepe paper cut with the grain of the crepe and wound tightly around and around a pencil.

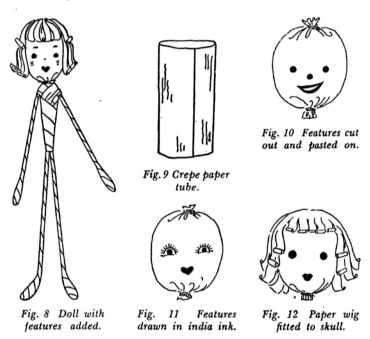

Fig. 9 Crepe paper tube.

Fig. 10 Features cut out and pasted on.

Fig. 8 Doll with features added.

Fig. 11 Features drawn in india ink.

Fig. 12 Paper wig fitted to skull.

Step 2. Make the body. Use one length of wire, note Figures 5 and 6 for the legs and body. At each end bend the wire into little loops for the feet. Wrap the full length of the wire [7] with a strip of crepe paper ¼ to 1-inch wide depending on the size of your doll. Wrap and rewrap it if necessary to get proper thickness. Bend the wire in the center.

Arms. Make them like the legs, but don't bend them in the center.

Step 3. Put the doll together. Tie the head, legs and body together with spool wire (*Fig. 6*). Tie arms to body with spool wire at center front directly under the head (*Fig. 8*). For a tiny favor doll, that's all there is to it. If your doll must have more body, cut a strip of crepe paper [1] about one inch wide, and wrap the body bandage fashion

See General Direction 1, *p.* 223; 7, *p.* 227

around and around stretching the crepe paper as you proceed and adding a tiny bit of paste now and again. The last wrapping can be in a color to serve as the bodice of the costume.

Step 4. Dress the doll. Costumes can be made of cloth or crepe paper. The latter is in general use. Basically all costumes are made much alike, variety being secured by detail. Remember, crepe paper can be pasted or sewn by hand or machine.

Following are the basic ideas of crepe paper costumes; some actual patterns are given in Chapter V.

Women's Costumes. Sleeves are tubes of crepe paper with the grain of the crepe running from the shoulder to the wrist. These tubes can be seamed with needle and thread or with paste. At the shoulders they can be gathered and pasted in place; at the wrists they can be tied with ribbons or with spool wire, or they can be pasted down.

Skirts are strips [1] of crepe paper gathered very full and tied or pasted around the waist. The grain of the crepe runs from the waist to the hem.

Bodices may be crepe paper strips [1] wrapped [7] around and around the the body and pasted only here and there to hold them in place, or they may be simple paper doll-like blouses pasted in place at the shoulders, under the arms, and possibly at the waist line. If the doll is large enough, the blouse may be made like any doll's blouse, cut and stitched, and tied or pasted at strategic points.

Collars are usually ruffles [15] of crepe paper gathered down the center length across the grain and pasted or tied in place.

Ruffle trims are widely used as edges on skirts, aprons, blouses, etc. They can be made additionally attractive by finger scalloping, [17] by fluting, [8] by twisted petals, [18] by lace edging.

Men's Costumes. Sleeves and trousers are tubes of crepe paper with the grain of the crepe running up and down the tubes. These tubes can be seamed with needle and thread or with paste and pasted in place at the shoulders and waist line.

Shirts, vests, coats are usually cut from patterns and pasted in position at the shoulders and, if necessary, under the arms. Patterns are given for a man's full-dress shirt, vest, and coat in Chapter II.

Hats. These are nearly always bits of crepe paper pasted together. Skull caps are the foundation for many of them. Because crepe paper can be stretched and cupped, all sorts of hats from berets, and over-seas caps to sombreros can be shaped from a simple skull cap. Directions for making the latter are given in Chapter VI.

See General Direction 1, *p.* 223; 7, *p.* 227; 15, *p.* 231; 17, *p.* 232; 3, *p.* 224; 18, *p.* 232

Step 5. How to anchor a wire doll in place. The feet can be bent and tied to a cardboard base with spool wire.

Tiny dolls can be seated on top of powder boxes and tied there with spool wire.

THE SECRET OF TYING GRACEFUL BOWS

CANDLES MAKE THE birthday cake. Pretty ribbon bows "make" a party favor or a gift package (*Fig. 13, 14* and *15*). Crunch a square of cellophane or tissue paper around some candies, tie it, add a really pretty bow and you have a favor.

Fig. 13 (Above) Fig. 14 (Below) and Fig. 15 (Right) Show how prettily a gift or favor can be wrapped.

Few people know how to tie such a bow. Professionals do it in three quick steps. Here they are.

Step 1. Form the loops holding the ribbon as illustrated (*Fig. 16*). Make as many loops as you wish. If the ribbon is wide enough gather it in at the center as you form the loops.

Step 2. Gather all of the loops in at the center (*Fig. 17*) and tie them with a short piece of ribbon or spool wire as described below.

Step 3. Pull bow into shape (*Fig. 18*). Cut ends of ribbon used for tying at smart angles.

How to Fasten a Bow with Spool Wire

Spool wire is used in making many bows for party favors and gift packages. There are two reasons: it helps make the bow perky, the spool wire ends are used to tie the bow in place.

This is the way to use spool wire:

Step 1. Form ribbon loops (*Fig. 16*).

 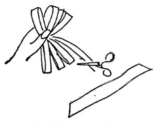

Fig. 16 Hold ribbon and form loops.

Fig. 17 Gather loops together and tie.

Fig. 18 Pull bow into shape.

Step 2. Cut the necessary length of spool wire, perhaps 8-inches. Double the wire making a hairpin shape. Place the loops within the hairpin curve (*Fig. 19*). Twist the wires firmly together in back and as close to the bow as possible (*Fig. 20*).

Step 3. Pull the bow into shape. Cut ends of ribbon at smart angles. Use the spool wire ends to tie the bow in place, or cut off the surplus wire and paste the bow in place.

How to Fasten a Bow to a Ribbon-Tied Package

This is the way it's done by experts in gift-wrapping departments.

Step 1. Tie the package (*Fig. 21*). Put a pin at X if necessary to hold it.

Step 2. Form loops (*Fig. 16* and *17*).

Fig. 19 Loops within hairpin curve.

Fig. 20 Wire twisted in middle of bow.

Step 3. Place loops on package and tie them with the ribbon ends (*Fig. 22*), or make bow as illustrated in Figures 19 and 20 and, with the spool wire ends, tie it to the ribbon on the package.

Bows that are Different

Turn out pretty bows for hats, corsages, dresses, party decorations and gift packages. Many women who can make exceptionally pretty bows, use their skill in business, especially in stores that feature gift wrapping departments. Here are some of the bows you can make. They are all based on the 3-step method shown in Figures 16, 17 and 18.

Two-tone Bows. Make loops of one color. Tie with spool wire (*Fig. 19 and 20*). Make second group of shorter loops in another color. Tie them to first group with a short length of ribbon. Some seasonal

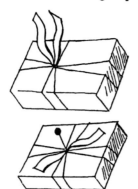

Fig. 21 (Left)
Package tied and
held with pin.

Fig. 22 Bow tied to package with ribbon ends.

color combinations are:

Winter—(Christmas) red and white; angel blue and cerise.

Spring—(Easter) purple and pale yellow; spring green and yellow.

Fall—orange and brown; emerald green and gold.

Summer—sea blue and green; daisy white and yellow.

Two-texture Bows. Make one set of loops of one kind of ribbon, the other of a different; for example, for Christmas, red satin and silver tinsel; for bridal packages, white satin and tulle; for children's gifts, paper and cellophane ribbons. Velvet and taffeta, satin and lace make handsome combinations.

Rosettes. Make many loops, tie them with spool wire, and cut some ends in V shape. To do that neatly, fold the ribbon ends in the center and cut ribbon at an angle.

Flat or Tailored Bows. Form loops of staggered length. Do not gather them in the center. Paste a flat piece of ribbon around the center. Paste or pin the bow in place.

Bows with Flower Centers. Tie bows the 3-step way, catching the short wire stem of a flower in with the spool wire or ribbon tie. With spool wire ties, other things besides flowers can be used for centers.

[108]

PROFESSIONAL SLANTS ON NUT OR CANDY CUPS

IF YOU WANT to know the basic facts about decorating nut cups in order that you may carry out your own color schemes, your own ideas, here they are. Home-makers who like to put originality into their entertaining will find these directions useful.

Where to Get the Foundation Cups

Paper soufflé or serving cups which are used as the foundations of party nut or candy cups can be bought at many chain, stationery or department stores. They can usually be had in four sizes running from a mere 1½-inches in diameter to 3¼-inches in diameter.

Fig. 23 Nut cup handle pasted to the outside.	*Fig. 24 Handle bent around cup's edge.*	*Fig. 25 Handle pasted to one side of nut cup.*

How to Make Handles

Attractive nut cups can be made with or without handles. Handles are often used as they offer one more point for decoration. A flower, a bow, a place card—or all three may be tied to the handle. Bells, stars, cupids, and other ready-made gummed seals can also be used.

When handles are used, they are usually put in place before the cups are covered.

No. 9 or 10 wire is the right weight for handles (see Wire Chart in Chapter XV). Cut it long enough to reach to the bottom of the cup. Before bending it to shape, wrap it twice ¹ with a ½-inch wide strip of crepe paper in the color selected. After wrapping it, bend it to the shape desired and fasten it to the outside of the cup with patches of gummed paper tape (*Fig. 23*).

See General Direction, 7, p. 227

Figures 24 and 25 show other ways of fastening the handles to the cup. When wire isn't available, handles can be made from Crepe Paper Twist.[19] Two or three strands of various hues can be twisted together to carry out color schemes.

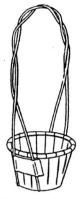  

Fig. 26 A two wire handle.	Fig. 27 Lattice type handle.	Fig. 28 Corkscrew handle.

Figure 23 shows the most widely used handle.

Figure 26 shows two wires. Each can be wrapped in a different color to carry out club, school or holiday color schemes.

Figure 27, a lattice-type handle, is often decorated with sprays of flowers or vines.

Figure 28, the corkscrew wire handle, is made by winding a No. 9 or 10 wire around a knitting needle. It is wrapped first with a strip of crepe paper [7] in the color desired. An interesting effect can be secured by wrapping the wire in two colors, adding the second one in spiral fashion candy-stick style so that the first shows through.

Figure 24 shows how a handle can be hooked through a cup.

Figure 25 shows another way of attaching a handle to a cup. When handles are fastened to the inside like this with gummed paper, a second cup can be placed inside the first to conceal the handle ends.

How to Cover Nut Cups

Basic Method (*Fig. 29*). Many, many cups are covered in this basic way, no matter how they are to be trimmed later. Cut a strip [1] of crepe paper across the grain ½-inch wider than the cup is high. Brush the outside of the cup lightly with paste. Stretch the strip around the cup and its brim. As you stretch the paper, its top edge will curl in and lie flat ¼-inch or more on the inside of the cup. If necessary,

See General Direction 19, *p.* 233; 7, *p.* 227; 1, *p.* 223

trim the lower edge even with the base of the cup. Paste down and overlap the two ends.

Twisted Petal Edge *(Fig. 30)*. Cut a strip [1] of crepe paper across the grain about 1-inch wider than the cup is high. Make a twisted petal edge.[18] Brush the outside of the cup lightly with paste and place the paper around it, letting it lie in slight gathers.

Curled Fringe Edge *(Fig. 31)*. This quick cover—kindergarten easy to make—can have its edge curled in *(Fig. 31)*, or out *(Fig. 32)*; it can have square tipped fringe or pointed tips. Both are shown in Figure 32. It can have fine or wide fringe. Through these simple variations and also combinations of colors, cups of widely different appearance can be made; for example, if the cup is covered first with

Fig. 29 *Basic covering method.*

Fig. 30 *Twisted petal edge.*

Fig. 31 *Curled petal edge.*

Fig. 32 *Curled fringe edge.*

Fig. 33 *Double ruffle edge.*

yellow blunt edged fringe, curled in, and then with green, cut into points and curled out, your cup will suggest a field daisy. To make this trim: cut a strip of crepe paper [1] about 1-inch wider than the cup is high. Along one edge slash it into fringe [2] about 1-inch deep. Curl the fringe over your scissor's blade.[5] Brush the outside of the cup lightly with paste. Place the crepe strip around it overlapping and pasting down the two ends. Trim the bottom edge if necessary.

Double Ruffle Edge *(Fig. 33)*. This easy-to-make cover and trim is a gem for carrying out a two-color combination for club, school, or holi-

See General Direction 1, *p.* 223; 18, *p.* 232; 2, *p.* 223; 5, *p.* 225

day season. Start by covering the cup by the Basic Method. To make the ruffle, cut a strip,[1] preferably in a different color, across the grain about 1½-inches wide. For each cup, cut off enough to go around the cup a little over two times. Fold and crease the strip in half along its length. Place a knitting needle inside the crease, then crush the paper together pushing it from both ends (*Fig. 34*). Slip a piece of spool wire (long enough to tie around the cup) in the

Fig. 34 Making the double ruffle edge.

Fig. 35 Machine gathered ruffle.

crease and tie the ruffle in place. Twist, don't knot, the spool wire ends. Adjust the fullness after you have the wire tied. A little paste added to the cup will keep the ruffle from slipping if the wire tie doesn't hold it.

Cellophane ruffle. This sparkles prettily. Make it like the Double Ruffle of crepe paper just described, tying it on with spool wire.

Machine Gathered Ruffle (*Fig. 35*). Cut a strip [1] of crepe paper about 1-inch wider than the cup is high. Machine gather it along one edge, about ¼ to ½-inch from the edge. Cut off enough to fit around the cup. Brush the outside of the cup very lightly with paste and place the ruffle in place overlapping and pasting down the ends. Two ruffles, each a different color, can be used attractively for this cup. Attractive, too, is a cup covered in one color by the Basic Method, and then with a Machine Gathered Ruffle pasted only along the bottom part of the cup. Ribbons with pretty bows can be tied around the stitching.

See General Direction 1, *p.* 223

CHAPTER V

How to Make Fancy Costumes for Plays, Pageants and Parties

"QUICK, THE COSTUME-BOOK!" Johnny must represent a bunny in the Sunday School Easter Pageant, or Little Sister is to be an angel in the Christmas Play.

"Quick, the costume-book!" You're going to a masquerade dance. What kind of a costume will you wear? How can you make it?

On the following pages you will find step-by-step directions for making those children's costumes most frequently requested by schools and churches for pageants, plays and other festivals; hints on making adult costumes; dramatic accessories for fancy costumes; instructions for making basic costumes which will give you a starting point for making any costume of your own design.

In this chapter, reference is occasionally made to the General Directions in Chapter XV. Unless you are familiar with handling crepe paper, be sure to look up the references. They are indicated by small numbers appearing to the right of directions; for example: "Cut a strip,¹" means to read General Direction 1.

What material will you use? The instructions in this book are based on the use of crepe paper for the following reasons:

It is the only material that can be curled, for example, to make a rose petal, slashed to imitate feathers, and so forth and so on and on and on.

Seventy-five cents is the average cost of an elaborate crepe paper costume. When numbers of costumes are being made at one time for a school or church affair, or when simple ones are made, the cost per costume is far less than that, sometimes only a few cents.

It comes in a wide range of colors and can be bought in the smallest community as well as in the largest city.

No dress patterns are required for crepe paper costumes. This is a rule with few exceptions.

If you can't sew—you can still make crepe paper costumes for they can be pasted together.

If you can sew—you can stitch your costumes just as you would if they were of cloth.

[113]

THE FAITHFUL FIVE—BASIC WAYS TO MAKE A COSTUME

HERE IS A BRIEF description of the five basic ways to make a crepe paper costume. Necessary details follow the descriptions.

Slip-Over Costume

The quickest way to turn out a costume is to use a "slip-over" (*Fig. 1*). This is kin to an apron, is slipped on over the head, and is worn over the child's dress or suit. Almost any costume can be made in this simplified way. Slip-overs are used probably ninety-nine times out of a hundred for school plays, pageants, etc.

Fig. 1   Slip-over
type of costume.

Fig. 2   Sandwich
man type of cos-
tume.

Fig. 3   Basic-top
type of costume.

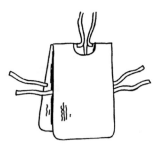

Fig. 4   One-piece
slip-over.

Sandwich Man Costume

These are cardboard cut-outs or posters tied over the shoulders, and worn, front and back, in sandwich man fashion (*Fig. 2*). These costumes are particularly practical for propaganda purposes. When a play, for example, is being given to teach school children certain health habits—sandwich men costumes are ideal. On the poster-like cut-outs, a big bottle of milk, tooth brushes, soap, carrots, beds can be depicted. Extra

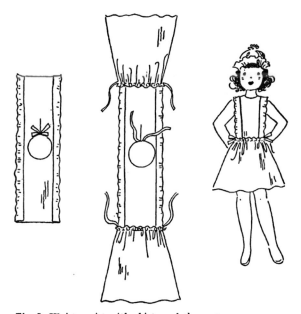

Fig. 5 Waist, waist with skirt, and the costume as worn.

touches can be added, if desired, by headbands, or caps. The Carrot Costume described in this chapter is a sandwich man costume elaborated upon.

Underwear-Foundation

Slightly more elaborate costumes than slip-overs are made right on a little girl's slip or a little boy's muslin shorts and shirt. The crepe paper is sewed or pasted to the old undergarment. If the costume is to be fringed or slashed, the undergarment should be of approximately the same color as the crepe paper. These underwear-foundation costumes which are widely used, are a great help to the woman who has no knack for sewing.

[115]

Basic-Top

This consists of a simple cotton top to which a crepe paper skirt is sewed, and over which a separate bodice of paper, cloth, or even of cardboard is worn (*Fig. 3*). It is especially useful for adult costumes.

Dressmaker Costume

For an extremely elaborate costume, one that is to be stored away in a dress bag and worn maybe annually, the entire foundation can be

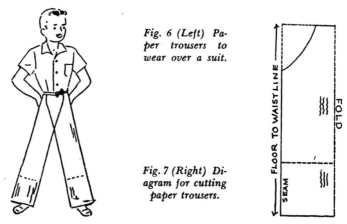

Fig. 6 (Left) Paper trousers to wear over a suit.

Fig. 7 (Right) Diagram for cutting paper trousers.

made of cloth, and intricate parts of the crepe paper costume can be cut by following a commercial tissue pattern. Such costumes are once-in-a-lifetime-if-then needs.

DETAILED INSTRUCTIONS FOR BASIC COSTUMES

BEFORE MAKING ANY of the costumes sketched in this chapter, or before making any crepe paper costumes of your own designing, it is well to familiarize yourself with the following information. Once you have this ground work in mind, it will be much easier to make any of the costumes described, and it will be fun to concoct designs of your own.

Slip-Overs

Slip-overs (*Fig. 1*) can be made in one-piece or two-piece style. The front and back are made alike and are usually trimmed alike.

ONE-PIECE SLIP-OVER

All that is necessary to make a one-piece slip-over is a straight piece of crepe paper long enough to reach from neck to skirt edge front and back, ribbons to tie the front and back together at the sides and the back

[116]

slit together at the neck (*Fig. 4*). This is as easy to make as a paper doll's dress.

Slip-overs can be varied to obtain quite different results.

Note the following suggestions.

For Halloween—make slip-over of orange crepe paper, tie it with black ribbons and trim it with black paper silhouettes of any of the Halloween symbols—cats, bats, witches.

For Valentine's Day—make slip-over of white crepe paper, tie it with red ribbons and trim it with red hearts and gold arrows cut from paper.

For Easter—make slip-over of yellow or orchid crepe paper, tie it with pale green ribbons and trim it with egg shaped cut-outs of brightly colored papers.

For Christmas—make slip-over of red crepe paper, tie it with red ribbon, trim it with white "cotton" snow—or sprays of holly—or tiny Christmas tree bells.

Two-Piece Slip-Over

To make the waist (*Fig. 5*) open up the fold of crepe paper. Cut off a piece twice as long as the child's waist. Fold it in two with the grain of

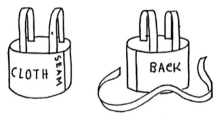

Fig. 8 Cotton band with shoulder straps.

the crepe and cut out an opening for the neck. Cut enough off along the sides to make the waist a generous shoulder width. Fold back 1-inch along each side, press the fold down with your fingers, and flute [*] the outside edge. This doubled edge along the sides of the waist not only gives a decorative trim, it also reinforces the sides to which the ribbons are sewed.

When a skirt is to be very full and heavy or a waist is to be decorated in various ways, it is often desirable to make the waist of two thicknesses of crepe paper stitching the two together around the edges.

To make the skirt (*Fig. 5*), cut the necessary length, with the grain of the crepe running from the waist to the skirt edge. Gather one length for the front, one for the back, and sew them in place.

See General Direction 3, *p.* 224

[117]

Underwear-Foundation

Girl's costumes. Sewing or pasting a girl's crepe paper costume to an old cotton slip presents no difficulties. Paste or sew it along the strategic seams. Remember that the grain of the crepe must run from the top of sleeve, waist, and skirt to the bottom.

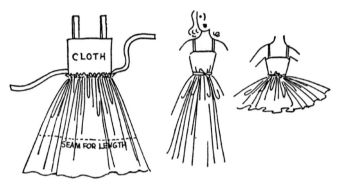

Fig. 9 Details for making the skirt. Grain of crepe must run from waist to skirt's edge.

Boy's costumes. (a) Trousers can be cut from crepe paper following a commercial tissue pattern, and then sewed or pasted along seams to an old pair of cotton shorts, or pajama pants.

(b) An easy way to make trousers of crepe paper which can be worn over a boy's cotton suit is shown in Figure 6. These can be worn only when the costume's top part, tunic, jacket or blouse, is hip length. For Indian, Chinese, Santa Claus, and many other costumes, they are satisfactory and practical. The tops of the trousers are sewed to a piece of cotton tape tied around the waist. To make them, proceed as follows:

Step 1. Take these measurements: (a) Waist. (b) Thigh at the fullest part. (c) Length from crotch to floor. (d) Length from waist to floor at side.

Step 2. Seam by stitching two 20-inch pieces of crepe paper together making a piece, therefore, 40-inches long. For width allow twice the thigh measurement plus 6-inches for fullness. Forty inches is an average length. Cut from it or add to it if necessary. Cut this seamed piece in two, lengthwise, to make two leg pieces. Fold each piece in two, lengthwise, and seam the edges.

Step 3. Measure from the bottom of the trouser leg to the crotch, then cut in a curved line as shown in Figure 7.

Tie a piece of tape around the boy's waist, put the trousers on and pin then sew them in place.

Basic-Top Costume

With this type of costume, a separate bodice is made to wear over the "camisole top." The bodice, often but not always of the basque type, may be made with the aid of a commercial pattern. The "Basic-Top" costume consists of a cloth top and a crepe paper skirt.

Top

Make a straight cotton band with shoulder straps (*Fig. 8*). It is most convenient not to seam this camisole top, but to leave it open, until you have stitched the crepe paper skirt to it. Sew a long length of cotton tape to the center back. This is used to tie around the waist to give a nipped in effect.

Skirt

Because the crepe paper is 20-inches wide, two widths must often be sewed together to get the necessary length (*Fig. 9*). The grain of the crepe must always run from waist to skirt's edge. For a child's skirt use, as a general rule for fullness, 1½-yards; for an adult's, 2½-yards.

CHILDREN'S COSTUMES

FOR PLAYS AND for parties here are attractive and symbolic costumes that you can make easily from crepe paper. For plays and pageants, it's fun, efficient, and economical to make them in mass production methods, one member of a committee cutting, another stitching, another assembling, etc.

Carrot Costume

This carrot (*Fig. 10*) is a sandwich man type of costume.

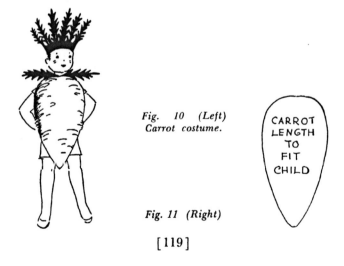

Fig. 10 (*Left*)
Carrot costume.

CARROT
LENGTH
TO
FIT
CHILD

Fig. 11 (*Right*)

[119]

Materials Needed to Make One:
1 fold crepe paper orange
1 fold crepe paper dark green
2 sheets cardboard light weight (color optional)
4 wires No. 9 or 10
Cloth tape, paste, glue or gummed paper tape, tissue paper, brown or black crayon

CARROT BODY

Step 1. Cut two pieces of your cardboard in carrot shape (*Fig. 11*). Pad one side of each with crushed tissue paper pasted in place.

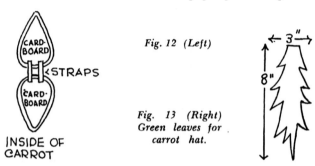

Fig. 12 (Left)

Fig. 13 (Right) Green leaves for carrot hat.

INSIDE OF CARROT

Step 2. Stretch your orange crepe paper until there is no stretch left in it. Cover each padded carrot with two thicknesses of it with the grain of the crepe running across the carrot. Paste it down neatly on the back side edges. Mark the carrot with its characteristic dark streaks using a brown or black crayon.

Step 3. Fasten two shoulder straps in place with gummed paper tape (*Fig. 12*).

CARROT HAT

Step 1. Make a 2-inch wide crown of cardboard to fit the child's head. Cover it with stretched green crepe pasted in place.

Step 2. Cut two strips of green leaves (*Fig. 13*) 3-inches wide at the widest point and 8-inches high.[13]

Step 3. Cut a No. 9 or 10 wire into 8-inch lengths and paste one down the center of each leaf on the strip.[11] Paste the other strip over the wired one. Use paste of a dry consistency and use it sparingly.

Step 4. Paste the leaves around the crown.

Step 5. Cut four more leaves, wire them in the same way, and paste them to the top of the carrot.

See General Direction 13, *p.* 229; 11, *p.* 229

Tomato Costume

This child's costume (*Fig. 14*) is made over an old slip.

Materials Needed to Make One:

3 folds crepe paper red
1 fold crepe paper dark green
1 No. 1 or 2 Spool Wire
1 wire No. 9 or 10
1¼ yards black elastic about ½-inch wide for head and shoe bands
⅓ yard red ribbon or tape to tie the costume at the neck
A straight slip, not ruffled, for the foundation. The slip should be 3-inches shorter than the finished costume.
Paste, tissue paper (color optional)

Use a whole fold of crepe for the tomato. When you put the costume together let the seam lie toward the top where the leaves will cover it.

 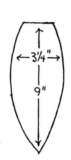 

Fig. 14 Tomato costume.	Fig. 15 Leaf shape for the costume.	Fig. 16 Leaf shape for the hat.

DRESS

Step 1. Gather one long edge of the red crepe on your sewing machine. Sew the gathered edge to the bottom, underside, of the slip with the ends slightly overlapping in the back.

Step 2. Turn the paper up and gather it along the top edge with needle and thread, drawing it to fit around the neck loosely.

Step 3. Cut openings at the sides for the arms, and paste or sew the edges to the slip's arm holes. Stuff crushed tissue paper between the paper and the slip to round the tomato out.

[121]

Step 4. Overlap and paste the crepe paper up the back leaving an opening of 4 or 5-inches for the neck.

Step 5. Following Figure 15, cut seven leaves from green crepe paper. Grain of crepe must run from tip to base. Paste these around the underside of the neck, gathering them slightly at the base to fit.

HAT

Step 1. Make an elastic headband. Cut four leaves [13] from green crepe paper following Figure 16. Paste a length of No. 9 or 10 wire [11] down the center of two. Then cover them with the other two leaves, pasting them in place. Use your paste very sparingly, and brush it on lightly with, not against, the grain of the crepe.

Step 2. Bend the leaves to shape and pin them to the headband.

SHOE BUCKLES

Step 1. Make two smaller leaves in the same way and paste them to elastic bands.

Ear of Corn Costume

This is a slip-over type of costume (*Fig. 17*).

Materials Needed to Make One:
2 folds crepe paper amber or yellow
1 fold crepe paper light green
1 fold crepe paper dark green
2 yards ½-inch wide green ribbon
1 spool wire No. 1 or 2
A flag stick or other round stick about ½-inch in diameter and 40-inches long.
Paste

DRESS

Step 1. Make a one-piece slip-over of two thicknesses of yellow crepe paper (*Fig. 4*), stitching the two together around all edges. Sew ribbons at sides and back of neck.

Step 2. Make kernels. Open up your fold of yellow crepe, and cut off from the end, two pieces, each 4-inches wide. These pieces will be 20-inches long. Join the two with paste to make a strip 40-inches long.

Step 3. Roll the strip around and around the flag stick (*Fig. 18*). Paste the edge down slightly. Place the end of the stick on a table or on the floor and push the crepe down hard (*Fig. 19*). Begin near the

See General Direction 13, *p.* 229; 11, *p.* 229

bottom and push down a small section at a time, gradually working up the stick until the entire roll is deeply crinkled.

Step 4. Slip the paper off the stick and stretch it out carefully to about 19-inches in length. Make nine of these rows of kernels.

Step 5. Paste the kernels in parallel rows to the front of the dress, turning the ends under at the top and bottom and pasting them down neatly.

Step 6. Back and sides. Cut six light green leaves; [18] eight dark green (*Fig. 20*).

Step 7. Paste four light green leaves, top edge only, to the back of the neck (*Fig. 21*). Paste two light green ones on each shoulder slightly overlapping the kernel section.

Step 8. Seam two dark green leaves (*Fig. 22*). Make four of these. Paste them over the shoulders so they fall to the front and back (*Fig. 17*).

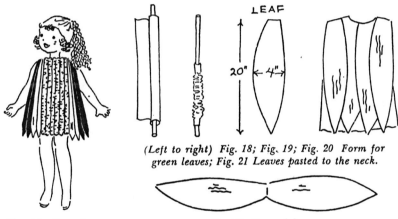

(*Left to right*) *Fig. 18; Fig. 19; Fig. 20 Form for green leaves; Fig. 21 Leaves pasted to the neck.*

Fig. 17 Ear of corn costume.

Fig. 22 Seamed leaves.

HAT

Step 1. Make a skull cap of yellow crepe paper. Steps in making a skull cap are given in Chapter VI. Cut the yellow crepe 12-inches wide across the grain of the crepe, and long enough to fit snugly around the child's head. Fold the strip in two, across the grain. Paste the short ends together slipping one inside the other. Gather the raw edges and tie them tightly with spool wire at the same time tying in some finely cut curly yellow fringe.[20] The fringe will hang in the inside of the cap like the tongue of a bell. Turn the cap inside out, so that the fringe will hang like a long tassel.

See General Direction 13, *p.* 229; 20, *p.* 234

Sun Costume

This is a slip-over type of costume (*Fig. 23*).

Materials Needed to Make One:
    1 fold crepe paper yellow
    1 fold crepe paper orange
    1 sheet cardboard
    2 yards gold foil paper
    3 yards narrow yellow ribbon
    ½ yard narrow elastic
    Paste

DRESS

Step 1. Make a one-piece slip-over of yellow crepe paper. Note Figure 4.

Step 2. Cut about ten sun motifs from orange crepe paper—making each on a 5-inch diameter circle as shown in Figure 24. Paste a circle of gold paper about 1½-inches in diameter in the center of each "sun."

Step 3. Paste the "suns" to the front and back of the yellow dress. Use the paste very sparingly and apply it with the grain.

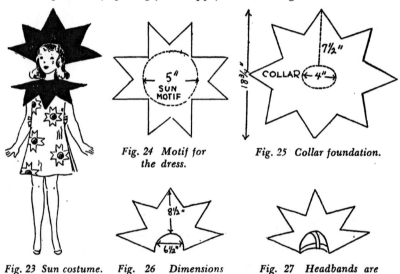

Fig. 24 Motif for the dress.

Fig. 25 Collar foundation.

Fig. 23 Sun costume.

Fig. 26 Dimensions for the headdress.

Fig. 27 Headbands are attached to the headdress.

COLLAR

Step 1. Cut a foundation from wrapping paper (*Fig. 25*). Cut it along the dotted lines.

Step 2. Cover the foundation with gold paper. Sew ribbon ties at the back opening. Bend the collar through the center over the shoulders.

HEADDRESS

This large headdress may be reduced for a very small child.

Step 1. Cut two pieces of cardboard of the size and shape shown in Figure 26.

Step 2. Cover both sides with shiny gold paper.

Step 3. Make bands of cardboard 1-inch wide. Cover them with gold paper and fasten them in place to fit the back of the head (*Fig. 27*).

Step 4. Sew elastic in place to form an under-chin strap to hold the headdress steady.

Fairy Costume

This is a two-piece slip-cover costume (*Fig. 28*).

Materials Needed to Make One:
3 folds crepe paper white
1 sheet white mat stock or lightweight cardboard
1 yard shiny silver paper
1 flag stick about 27-inches long
1 wire No. 1 or 2
4 wires No. 7 or 15
Small gummed silver stars, white gauze ribbon
Paste

DRESS

Step 1. Make the waist as described previously under "Slip-Over Costumes, Two-Piece" (*Fig. 5*).

Step 2. To make the skirts, cut three strips[1] of crepe paper and cut each, along one edge, into points.[13] Gather the top edge of each on the machine making the shortest of the three the fullest.

Step 3. Cut off sufficient lengths for the skirt, front and back.

Step 4. Sew the skirts in place. Trim the points with silver gummed stars and sew ribbons to the sides as ties.

COLLAR

Step 1. Cut a strip[1] of white crepe paper 5-inches wide across the grain of the crepe and three times the length of the neck measurement.

Step 2. Cut it into points along one edge and gather the other on the

See General Direction 1, p. 223; 13, p. 229

sewing machine. This step may be done by hand.

Step 3. Add some small gummed silver stars and stitch it in place.

WINGS

Step 1. Make a wire foundation for each wing using the oval shape described in Chapter VI, Fairy and Bee Wings.

Step 2. Cover each wing with stretched white crepe paper and dot them with silver stars. Fasten them to the costume with narrow white ribbons.

CROWN

Step 1. Make a 2-inch deep headband of cardboard.

Step 2. Cover it with silver paper and top it, in tiara fashion, with silver stars pasted, front and back, to wires which have been wrapped [7] with crepe paper and gum taped to the crown.

WAND

Step 1. Wrap [7] your flag stick several times with white crepe paper, cut 1-inch wide across the grain.

Step 2. Tack two silver stars, back to back, to the top and tie a bow and shower of narrow white ribbons under the star.

Fig. 28 (Left)
Fairy costume.

Fig. 29 (Center)
Elf costume.

Fig. 30 (Above)
Pointed cap outline.

Elf Costume

The tunic of this costume (*Fig. 29*) is made slip-over style; the pants, over cotton shorts.

See General Direction 7, *p.* 227

Materials Needed to Make One:
1 fold crepe paper yellow
1 fold crepe paper green
Narrow green ribbon
Pair of old cotton shorts
Paste

TUNIC

Step 1. Make this in slip-over style (*Fig. 4*) of double thickness yellow crepe paper. Cut the bottom edge into points, and stitch the two thicknesses together at the sides. Cut a 4-inch slit down the back and sew on tie ribbons. ·

Step 2. Cut a 5-inch wide strip[1] of green crepe paper. Cut one edge into V shape petals;[13] gather the other and sew it around the neck.

BELT

Step 1. Make it of green crepe paper folded along the grain to several thicknesses. You may have to piece the crepe to get the necessary length. Fasten it with a safety pin or snap fasteners.

PANTS

Step 1. Cut a strip[1] of green crepe paper slightly longer than the boy's shorts which should be short indeed. Along one edge cut it into points.[13]

Step 2. Cover the cotton shorts with the crepe paper, cutting and sewing it where necessary.

HAT

Step 1. Cut two pieces of green crepe paper 11 by 12-inches with the grain of the crepe paper running the 12-inch length. Cut it into a pointed cap as shown in Figure 30. Stitch the sides together, and sew a tiny bell to the point. Turn back a narrow cuff and stretch it to a little flare.

Indian Costume for Boy

This costume (*Fig. 31*) is made over an underwear foundation.
Materials Needed to Make One:
2 folds crepe paper brown
1 fold crepe paper yellow
1 fold crepe paper red
1 fold crepe paper black

See General Direction 1, *p.* 223; 13, *p.* 229

1 fold crepe paper white
5 wires No. 9 or 10
An old pajama, two piece suit
Paste

TROUSERS

Follow the instructions given previously in this chapter regarding underwear-foundation, noting Figures 6 and 7. Make the trousers of brown crepe paper.

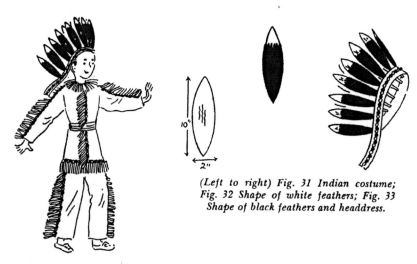

(*Left to right*) *Fig. 31 Indian costume; Fig. 32 Shape of white feathers; Fig. 33 Shape of black feathers and headdress.*

TUNIC

Step 1. Cut brown crepe paper to cover the sleeves, back, and front of the pajama jacket. The grain of the crepe runs from the top of the sleeves and jacket to the bottom.

Step 2. Sew or paste the sections to the jacket's seams.

Step 3. Paste straight crepe paper fringe in position. Make it by cutting a strip of crepe paper 6-inches wide across the grain and slashing it into straight fringe.[2] At the top of the fringe, paste red and yellow crepe paper beading.[32]

HEADDRESS

Step 1. Across the grain of your white crepe paper cut a strip 11-inches[1] wide. Following Figure 32, make a paper pattern.

Step 2. Cut a quantity of white feathers. You'll need twice as many as

See General Direction 2, p. 223; 32, p. 240; 1, p. 223

are required to fit around the wearer's head because each feather is double. Cut the feathers.[18]

Step 3. Paste a No. 9 or 10 wire [11] down the center of half of the feathers. Paste the other half of the feathers over the wired ones.

Step 4. Following Figure 33 cut black feathers from crepe paper. As these are not made double, you'll need only half as many as of the white ones.

Step 5. Paste a black feather lightly to the base of each white one.

Step 6. Stitch the feathers to a band of brown crepe paper made of several thicknesses folded with the grain of the crepe. You'll have to piece the paper to get the necessary length. Trim the band with yellow and red beading.[32]

BELT

Make this by folding crepe paper with the grain to several thicknesses. You may have to piece it to get enough length. Fasten the belt with a wee safety pin, or sew snaps to it.

Blue Bird Costume—for Boy or Girl

This is made over an underwear-foundation (*Fig. 34*). Other bird costumes can be made in the same way. Change the color scheme and there's a different bird!

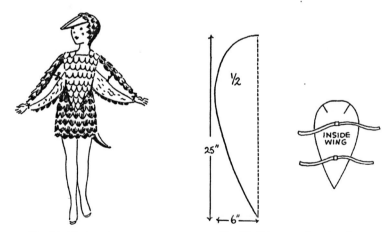

Fig. 34 Bird costume.   Fig. 35 Diagrams for the wings.

See General Direction 13, *p.* 229; 11, *p.* 229; 32, *p.* 240

Materials Needed to Make One:
> 4 folds crepe paper blue
> 1 fold crepe paper rose for the breast
> 1 yard glazed paper black
> 3 yards cotton fabric white or blue for the tail and wing foundations
> (buckram is fine, but a part of an old sheet will do)
> Narrow ribbon or white cotton tape
> 3 or 4 wires No. 9 or 10
> An old sleeveless blouse and shorts for a foundation
> Paste

PANTS

Step 1. Cut a strip [1] of blue crepe paper 3½-inches wide. Cut the strip into petal divisions [13] each 1-inch wide and 2½-inches deep.

Step 2. Beginning at the botton of a leg, sew the feathers on in overlapping rows, alternating them so that the feathers in one row lie between those in the previous row. Completely cover the pants.

TUNIC

Step 1. Cover the blouse with blue feathers just as you covered the pants, but paste several rows of rose feathers to the center front to represent the breast. The blouse should be no wider over the hips than is necessary to get it on over the child's head.

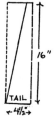

Fig. 36 *(Left) Diagram for the tail.*
Fig. 37 *(Center) Diagram of skull cap.*
Fig. 38 *(Right) Diagram for beak.*

WINGS

Step 1. Cut two pieces of fabric *(Fig. 35)*. Note and cut the darts at the shoulders. Outline the edges with No. 9 or 10 wire catching it down with needle and thread.

Step 2. Line each with crushed [16] blue crepe paper pasting it in place.

Step 3. Sew ribbons or tape to the inside of the wings to tie them around the arms and wrists.

Step 4. Fit the wings to the child's shoulder by overlapping them as much as necessary at the top darts. Paste the darts together.

See General Direction 1, *p.* 223; 13, *p.* 229; 16, *p.* 232

Step 5. Cover the outside of the wings with overlapping blue feathers starting at the bottom.

Step 6. Sew the wings to the shoulders of the blouse. Cover the stitches with an additional row of feathers, pasting them in place.

TAIL

Step 1. Cut a piece of fabric (*Fig. 36*). Outline the edges with No. 9 or 10 wire.

Step 2. Line the inside and cover the outside just as you did the wings, but include at the tip of the tail two or three extra long feathers.

Step 3. Sew the tail in place. Cover the stitches if necessary with a few extra feathers.

HEAD

Step 1. Make a blue skull cap 8-inches deep. Step-by-step directions are given at the end of Chapter VI. Cut the lower edge as shown in Figure 37.

Step 2. From double shiny black paper cut a beak following Figure 38.

Step 3. Fasten it to the front of the hat. Stitch, paste, or staple it on.

Step 4. Beginning at the lower edge of the cap, sew on overlapping rows of feathers cut from 2-inch wide strips of crepe paper—each "feather" 1-inch wide, 1½-inches deep.

Bunny Costume

This costume (*Fig. 39*) is made over an underwear-foundation. Not only a rabbit, but all sorts of animal costumes can be made in this very simple way by varying the colors and the headdress. A lion, for example, could be represented with a yellow body and long shaggy brown fringe collar and a tail tip. The tail can be made of wire wrapped [7] with crepe paper. Cardboard masks add to the realistic appearance of some animal costumes.

Materials Needed to Make One:
5 folds crepe paper white
1 fold crepe paper pink
1 wire No. 1 or 2
1 wire No. 9 or 10
An old one-piece pair of pajamas
Paste

BODY

Step 1. Completely cover the pajamas with finely crushed [16] white crepe

See General Direction 7, *p.* 227; 16, *p.* 232

[131]

paper, sewing the paper along the seams and catching it down here and there to hold it in place.

Step 2. Trim the neck, wrists, ankles with fluffy white crepe paper fringe made like this: Cut [1] strip of crepe paper 6-inches wide. Along each edge slash it into fine straight fringe.[2] Lay four strips together and gather them through the center with needle and thread.

Step 3. Sew the fringe in place and brush it briskly with your palm.

Step 4. Make a pompon of the same fringe [28] and sew it to the back of the costume for the tail.

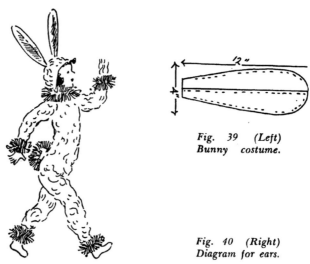

Fig. 39 (Left)
Bunny costume.

Fig. 40 (Right)
Diagram for ears.

HEADDRESS

Step 1. Make a tight-fitting, white crepe paper skull cap. See the directions at the end of Chapter VI.

Step 2. Make the ears as follows: Cut two pieces of white crepe paper and two pieces of pink (*Fig. 40*) with the grain of the crepe running from the tip of the ear to its base.

Step 3. Place a pink and white ear together, fold them lengthwise through the middle, lay a piece of No. 9 or 10 wire in the crease and stitch close to the wire on each side.

Step 4. Stitch around the edge of the ear, too. Turn up a short hem at the bottom of each ear, fold a little pleat in place, and then, with the pink forming the inside, sew the ears in place.

Step 5. Cover the skull cap with crushed white crepe paper, sewing or pasting it in place.

See General Direction 1, *p.* 223; 2, *p.* 223; 23, *p.* 235

Rose Costume

This rose (*Fig. 41*) is made over a child's slip.

Materials Needed to Make One:

2 folds crepe paper pink or rose
1 fold crepe paper green (Optional: a second fold of a different shade of green. See the section on the Bodice which follows).
1 No. 1 or 2 spool wire
An old cotton slip
Paste

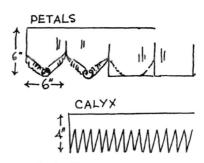

Fig. 41 (Left) Rose costume; Fig. 42 (Upper right) Diagram for the skirt; Fig. 43 (Lower right) Diagram for the bodice.

SKIRT

Step 1. From pink crepe paper cut an 8-inch wide strip 36-inches long.[1] Open up the strip, refold it to three thicknesses (8-inches by 12-inches) and cut it into a strip of petals 6-inches wide, and 6-inches deep [18] (*Fig. 42*). Open up the strip and curl-and-crush the corners of the petals over a pencil.[5] Gather the strip slightly.

Step 2. Make enough such petal strips to cover the skirt with three rows. Make each row narrower and skimpier than the previous. Each petal strip can be made of two different shades of pink, with the darker underneath. It isn't necessary to paste or sew the two strips together.

Step 3. Starting with the bottom row, sew or paste the petal strips to the slip's skirt.

BODICE

This is designed to represent a rose's calyx.

Step 1. From green crepe paper, cut a strip [1] about 4-inches wide. Open

See General Direction 1, *p.* 223; 18, *p.* 232; 5, *p.* 225

it up and refold it with the grain to not more than eight thicknesses. Along one edge cut it into points [18] (*Fig. 43*).

Step 2. Cut enough such strips to cover the top of the slip.

Step 3. Starting at the bottom of the waist sew on row after overlapping row. At the neck line, turn the last row under and stitch or paste the edges down. Each row can be made an alternating shade of green. Also, a large rose pinned to the shoulder, is a pretty touch.

CAP

Step 1. Make a skull cap of pink crepe paper following the directions given at the end of Chapter VI.

Step 2. Cover it with overlapping pink petals.

Step 3. To the top of the cap tie several rose leaves with an 8-inch length of spool wire.[6] Wrap the wire ends with a narrow strip of green crepe paper.[7] See Chapter I for making rose leaves.

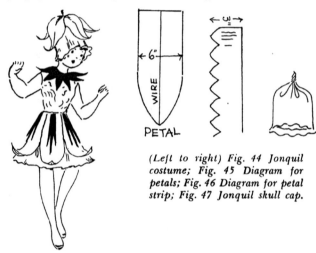

(Left to right) Fig. 44 Jonquil costume; Fig. 45 Diagram for petals; Fig. 46 Diagram for petal strip; Fig. 47 Jonquil skull cap.

Jonquil Costume

This jonquil (*Fig. 44*) is made over a child's slip.

Materials Needed to Make One:

1 fold crepe paper light yellow
1 fold crepe paper dark yellow
1 fold crepe paper green
1 wire No. 1 or 2
3 or 4 wires No. 9 or 10

See General Direction 18, *p.* 232; 6, *p.* 226; 7, *p.* 227

An old cotton slip or foundation
Paste

Skirt

Step 1. Gather a full skirt of dark yellow crepe paper, and sew it to the child's slip. Remember, the grain of the crepe must run from the waist to the bottom of the skirt.

Step 2. Following Figure 45, cut twelve light yellow petals.[13] Paste a wire down the center length of six,[11] and cover the six with the remaining petals.

Step 3. Cut six long pointed leaves from green crepe paper with the grain of the crepe running from tip to base.

Step 4. Paste these at the top of the petals.

Step 5. Sew the petals and leaves to the skirt top.

Waist

Step 1. Cover the top of the slip with dark yellow crushed [16] crepe paper sewing or pasting it down along the seams and here and there to hold it in place.

Step 2. Cut a strip of light yellow petals,[13] gather them slightly and sew or paste them around the neck line (*Fig. 46*).

Hat

Step 1. Make a skull cap of dark yellow crepe paper, cutting it deep enough to give the bell shape of the jonquil's center (*Fig. 47*). In making it, follow the directions given for skull caps at the end of Chapter VI. Turn the bottom edge under about ½-inch and flute [3] the doubled edge.

Step 2. Cut 12 petals of light yellow about 4-inches wide and 8-inches long. Wire them to make six, just as you did for the skirt.

Step 3. Paste a few pointed green leaves to the base of the petals and then tie them around the top of the skull cap with a 12-inch length of spool wire.[6]

Step 4. Wrap [7] the ends of the spool wire with a narrow strip of green crepe paper, thus forming a stem. Curl [5] the ends of all the petals over a scissors blade.

Daisy Costume

This costume (*Fig. 48*) is made over a cotton slip.

See General Direction 13, *p.* 229; 11, *p.* 229; 16, *p.* 232; 3, *p.* 224; 6, *p.* 226; 7, *p.* 227; 5, *p.* 225

Material Needed to Make One:
    1 fold crepe paper yellow
    1 fold crepe paper green
    2 folds crepe paper white
    1 wire No. 1 or 2
    An old cotton slip for a foundation
    Paste

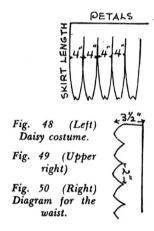

Fig. 48 (Left) Daisy costume.

Fig. 49 (Upper right)

Fig. 50 (Right) Diagram for the waist.

Skirt

Step 1. Gather a full skirt of yellow crepe paper with the grain running from the waist to the skirt's edge.

Step 2. Cut a strip[1] of white crepe paper to make the white skirt petals. Your petals should be 1-inch shorter than the skirt and you'll need, for fullness a strip of them 1½ times the waist measurement. Following Figure 49, cut the strip into petal shapes[13] with each petal division about 4-inches wide.

Step 3. Gather this and sew it around the waist.

Waist

Step 1. Cut a strip[1] of green crepe paper 3½-inches wide. Open it up, refold it to not more than eight thicknesses and cut it into a strip of leaf shapes[13] following Figure 50.

Step 2. Starting at the bottom of the waist sew or paste on row after overlapping row of the green leaves with the points in each row falling between those of the previous row.

Step 3. Add a few short rows across the shoulders. Finish the neckline smoothly by turning the crepe paper under and stitching or

See General Direction 1, *p.* 223; 13, *p.* 229

pasting it to the inside of the slip. Both methods have proved to be satisfactory.

HAT

Step 1. Make a shallow skull cap of dark yellow crepe paper following directions given at the end of Chapter VI.

Step 2. Cut a strip [1] of white crepe 8-inches wide, and 9-inches long.

Step 3. Following Figure 49, cut it into a strip of petals.[18] With spool wire, tie [6] the strip around the top of the hat.

Step 4. Cut a strip [1] of green crepe paper 4-inches wide and 7-inches long. Following Figure 49 cut it into a petal strip and tie it over the white petals.

Step 5. Wrap [7] the surplus crepe at the top of the hat with a narrow strip of green crepe.

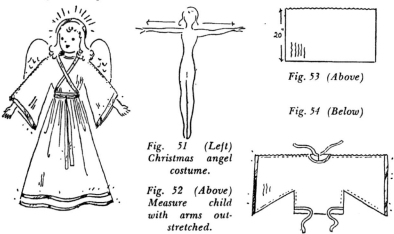

Fig. 53 (Above)

Fig. 54 (Below)

Fig. 51 (Left) Christmas angel costume.

Fig. 52 (Above) Measure child with arms outstretched.

Christmas Angel

This is a simply made costume (*Fig. 51*) for one-time wear. Although the wings must be made of crepe paper, the costume itself could be made, with minor changes, of heavy cheese cloth. The top is cut like a paper doll's kimona-style dress. The high waisted skirt is separate.

Materials Needed to Make One:
 2 folds crepe paper white
 1 fold crepe paper pale blue
 10 yards silver paper ribbon about 3/4-inch wide
 3 yards silver rayon ribbon about 1/2-inch wide
 2 or 3 wires No. 7 or 15 for wings

See General Direction 1, *p.* 223; 18, *p.* 232; 6, *p.* 226; 7, *p.* 227

1 No. 1 or 2 Spool wire for wings
Cardboard, a 9-inch square for halo
Silver foil paper to cover it
12 inches of elastic for halo
Pinking shears

BLOUSE

Step 1. Measure the child with her arms outstretched from one wrist to another. Note Figures 52, 53 and 54. Cut two pieces of crepe paper the length just taken using, if possible, pinking shears.

Step 2. Lay one piece over the other with the pinked edges matching.

Step 3. Cut an opening for the head, a 5-inch slit down the center back, and the outline of the sleeves.

Step 4. From pale blue crepe paper, cut 6-inch bands with which to line the bottom of each sleeve. Lay the linings in place.

Step 5. Stitch silver paper ribbon around the bottom of the sleeves and around the neck.

Step 6. On the machine stitch the sleeves, underarm seams, and the shoulder-to-wrist seams leaving on the latter a pinked-edge heading of about $1/4$-inch.

Step 7. To the back of the neck sew tie ribbons, and to the blouse, at the waist line, sew cotton tape leaving long ends to tie in front.

SKIRT

Step 1. Measure off enough crepe paper to make a moderately full skirt, $2\frac{1}{2}$ times the child's waist measure will be about right. If the skirt has to be more than 20-inches long, cut another piece and join the two on the sewing machine to get the necessary length. The grain of the crepe runs from waist to skirt's edge.

Step 2. Around the bottom edge, sew at least one row of silver paper ribbon.

Step 3. Gather the other edge to waist measurement.

Step 4. Make a center back seam and sew a snug white ribbon belt to the top. Put hooks and eyes on the belt.

WINGS

Step 1. Construct the wings by following the directions in Chapter VI for making Angel and Cupid Wings, covering them with white crepe paper feathers.

Step 2. Cut two 54-inch lengths of silver fabric ribbon. Sew one firmly at each side of the joining between the wings. Hold the wings in place on the costumed child. Criss-cross the ribbons in front, bring

[138]

them around the waist in back, then to the front, and tie them with a bow and streamers.

HALO

Step 1. Cut a cardboard circle about 8½-inches in diameter.

Step 2. One inch from the outside edge, cut out the center.

Step 3. Cover the halo, both sides, with silver paper.

Step 4. Punch holes in the sides and fasten elastic through them. The elastic must be short enough to hold the halo on.

You can let your imagination fly when you costume little novelty dolls made of wire and paper. Directions for making Novelty Dolls are on Page 102. The dolls in the photograph are used as place cards.

CHAPTER VI

Dramatic Costume Accessories You Can Make

HUGE FLOWER HEADDRESSES, wigs, wings and hats are just a few of the accessories—important for amateur theatricals, fun for parties—which you can make from crepe paper with the directions that follow.

OVER SIZE FLOWER HEADDRESSES

IMAGINE A PARADE of girls in simple white dresses or robes each with a fantastically large flower framing her face. It's a dramatic and sentiment-packed way of costuming girls for a floral pageant. Diagrams and instructions are given below for making a Daisy and a Lily Headdress. From these you can devise your own patterns and designs for headdresses depicting the iris, tiger lily, jonquil, rose, and other favorite blossoms.

Daisy Headdress

Designed for applause this over size daisy (*Fig. 1*) is reminiscent of the Ziegfeld Girl costumes. For a mere doll size child its theatrical dimensions might be whittled down a trifle.

Fig. 1 Daisy headdress.

Material Needed to Make One Headdress:

    1 fold Duplex crepe paper two-tone yellow
    1 fold Duplex crepe paper two-tone green
    1 fold crepe paper brown
    ⅔ yard orange ribbon ½-inch wide
    1 wire No. 1 or 2
    Paste, cardboard or wrapping paper for patterns

NOTE: *If you can't buy Duplex crepe you can always make your own by pasting two layers of crepe paper together.*

Step 1. Cap. Make a double skull cap from green Duplex with the lighter shade on the inside. Follow the step-by-step directions for making skull caps given at the end of this chapter.

Step 2. Flower. Open up your fold of brown crepe paper. Cut off with the grain a piece 3½-inches wide. It will be 20-inches long. Join to it, lightly with paste, another piece to give a length of 29-inches. Along one 29-inch side, slash it 2-inches deep at 1-inch intervals. This will give you a widely spaced curly fringe.[20]

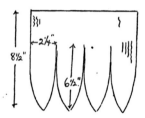

| Fig. 2 Diagram for petals forming daisy headdress. | Fig. 3 Brown fringe pasted to daisy petal strip. | Fig. 4 Diagram for green petals on daisy headdress. |

Cut across the grain of the two-tone yellow Duplex a strip [1] 8½-inches wide and 29-inches long. Make a pattern [12] following the dimensions of the petals in Figure 2. Using it as a guide, cut [13] the 29-inch strip into petals.

    Paste the strip of fringe to the base of the petals on the darker yellow side (*Fig. 3*). This is the side of the petals that will frame the face.

Step 3. Now paste the petals around the outside edge of the cap, leaving a few free at each end to be tied with orange ribbons under the chin.

Step 4. Guided by Figure 4, make a wrapping paper pattern. From green

See General Direction 20, *p.* 234; 1, *p.* 223; 12, *p.* 229; 13, *p.* 229

Duplex crepe cut a strip across the grain 3½-inches wide and 24-inches long. Using your pattern cut a strip of points to fit around the cap.

Step 5. Paste them along the edge only to the base of the yellow petals, with their points toward the top of the cap.

Step 6. Wrap [7] the very top of the cap, the part tied by spool wire, with a narrow strip of green crepe.

When the hat is worn, curl the petals back from the face like a gigantic halo.

Lily Headdress

This Alice in Wonderland size headdress (*Fig. 5*) may steal the show! Good drama for any play or pageant, it is most effective when worn with a completely simple dress or robe.

Fig. 5 Lily headdress.

Material Needed to Make One Headdress:

 2 folds Duplex crepe paper white
 1 fold Duplex crepe paper two-tone green
 1 fold crepe paper yellow
 1 fold crepe paper white
 1 yard narrow ribbon white
 12 wires No. 9 or 10
 Paste, wrapping paper to make patterns.

NOTE: *If you can't buy Duplex, or double thickness crepe paper you can always make your own by pasting two layers together.*

Step 1. Cap. Make a double skull cap of white crepe paper. Directions follow at end of chapter.

Step 2. Flower. Following the dimensions given in Figure 6, cut a pattern [12] of wrapping paper. From white Duplex crepe, cut three

---

See General Direction 7, *p.* 227; 12, *p.* 229

of these double petals, six points in all. These petals are an exception to the rule that the grain of the crepe must run from base to tip. On these it must from side to side.

Cut six No. 9 or 10 wires 22-inches long. Wrap each one with a narrow strip of white crepe paper.[7] Paste a wire down the center length of each petal.[11]

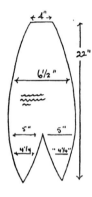

Fig. 6 *(Left) Diagram for petals forming lily headdress.*

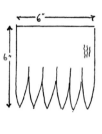

Fig. 7 *(Right) Diagram for calyx-like petals for lily headdress.*

Step 3. Pistils. (Note these pencil-like protrusions over the bangs in Figure 5). Cut six No. 9 or 10 wires 18-inches long. Wrap [7] each with a strip of green crepe paper. Cut across the grain of the crepe a strip [1] of yellow crepe 1½-inches wide. Wrap the end only of each wire to pencil thickness with the yellow. Tie the green ends of the pistils to the top of the skull cap with spool wire so that the yellow ends will extend beyond the child's forehead.

Step 4. Note side view of hat in Figure 5. Lightly paste the petals to the skull cap starting with the top ones. It's well to try the hat on at this point putting the petals in place carefully as indicated by the sketch. Tie the ends of the petals together with spool wire.[6] Add paste to the edges of the petals, overlap them, and press the sides together.

Step 5. Calyx. The side view of this headdress, shows a calyx shape at the lily's base. From ordinary wrapping paper make a pattern following the diagram in Figure 7. Using it as a guide, cut enough green Duplex petals [13] to paste around the base of the flower. Cut off any surplus crepe. On the calyx, the grain of the crepe runs from tip to base.

Sew narrow white ribbons to each side of the flower so it may be tied

See General Direction 7, *p.* 227; 11, *p.* 229; 1, *p.* 223; 6, *p.* 226; 13, *p.* 229

under the chin. Bend the wired petals up and away from the child's face.

WINGS FOR COSTUMES

WITH CREPE PAPER and wire it is easy to construct wings for all sorts of costumes from fairies to butterflies. Figures 8, 9, and 10 show the three most useful ways of making wings.

(Left to right) Fig. 8 Angel and cupid wings; Fig. 9 Fairy and bee wings; Fig. 10 Butterfly wings.

Angel and Cupid Wings

The wing shown in Figure 8 is especially appropriate for angels and cupids. Each wing is cut separately from lightweight cardboard, and then is reinforced with a heavy No. 7 or 15 wire which is held down with patches of gummed tape (*Fig. 11*).

After you have made two such frames, cover each side of the two with crepe paper, stretching it over the wires and pasting it down along the edges. Then cover the wings with feathers. What are the feathers? They are merely strips of crepe paper cut along one edge into pointed divisions.

To make the feathers, cut a strip [1] of crepe paper. Then cut it into "a strip of petals." [13] In pasting on the feathers (petals), start at the bottom of the wing, and add row after row, around and around the wings, overlapping each and arranging them so that the points of the feathers in one row lie between those of the previous row. If the edges of the wings seem to need it, paste individual feathers to them.

To fasten the wings in place, bend and sew the extension tabs (*Fig. 11*) to the costume. When the wings are heavy they can have ribbons taped to them, and the ribbons can be tied over the child's shoulders or criss-crossed over the front of the bodice and tied around the waist.

See General Direction 1, *p.* 223; 13, *p.* 229

Fairy and Bee Wings

These wings (*Fig. 9*) are widely used for bees and fairies. They are made of No. 7 or 15 wire bent to shape. (See Wire Chart). The ends are twisted together to join the two wings. The joining is made secure by wrapping spool wire tightly around and around it.

Before bending the wires to shape, wrap each one [7] with a strip of crepe paper cut about ½-inch across the grain.

These wings may be left uncovered or they may be covered with cellophane, tissue paper, or stretched crepe paper. If you cover them, cover each side pasting the material to the wrapped wire. If you use cellophane, glue is the adhesive to hold it to the wrapped wires. Paste is the adhesive for tissue or crepe paper. Sew these wings to the costume. Tie them, too, over the shoulders if necessary.

Fig. 11 (Left) Wing reinforced with wire.

Fig. 12 (Right) Butterfly wing completed.

Butterfly Wings

These are wings (*Fig. 10*) constructed like the wings in Figure 9. After wrapping the wires with crepe paper, bend them to the shape sketched. Cover both sides of each with stretched crepe paper. The easiest way to do it is to apply the paste to the wires, lay them on the crepe paper, then trim and press down the edges. No harm done if it isn't a spanking neat job!

After covering them completely, cut a smaller wing shape of another color. Paste it down lightly on the inside edge only, and paste on colored paper cut-outs (*Fig. 12*). Sew these wings to the costume.

Bird Wings

These are made on a muslin or buckram foundation. Complete instructions for making these wings are given in the section on the Blue Bird costume on Page 130 in Chapter V. Follow the directions given there and you will find these wings are easy to make. You can fit the wings to the shoulder by overlapping them as much as necessary at the top darts. Feathers can be as varied in color as the colorful birds they represent.

See General Direction 7, *p.* 227

WIGS OF CREPE PAPER

THE FOUNDATION OF these wigs is a skull cap made of an old piece of knitted cotton underwear or of crepe paper. See steps for making skull cap at the end of this chapter.

(Left to right) Fig. 13 Colonial coiffure; Fig. 14 Skull cap for colonial coiffure; Fig. 15 Dutch braid. Fig. 16 Short hair.

Colonial Coiffure

The method used for making this wig (*Fig. 13*) can be used for other up-swept hairdo's. Shape the bottom edge of a skull cap as shown in Figure 14. Hem the bottom and run an elastic through the hem. Tie it tightly to fit the headsize.

Make the hair itself of crushed crepe paper [16] pasting it, or catching it down to the foundation with needle and thread. Rolls, puffs and high pompadours may be made by padding the crushed crepe with wadding of crumbled tissue paper or cotton.

Curls. Cut along the grain of the crepe a strip 4-inches wide. With it, make a crushed crepe paper tube.[31] Remove the crushed tube from the stick, stretch it out slightly and cut it off into curl lengths. Paste or sew the curls to the cotton or paper skull.

Dutch Braids

Widely used for Dutch costumes, these braids (*Fig. 15*), of course, are suitable for many characters. They also make delightful playtime accessories for little girls. The child with short dark hair, for example, will love to have a long blonde wig for dressing-up play.

To Make the Hair. Make, first, a tight fitting skull cap of old knitted underwear or a stocking top. See the step-by-step directions for making skull caps at the end of this chapter. Then make the hair of soft curly fringe [20] leaving a heading of not more than ¾-inch. Stretch

See General Direction 16, *p.* 232; 31, *p.* 239; 20, *p.* 234

the fringe and cut it to the desired length. Goldilocks might have 18-inch locks. Stitch one length of fringe along the heading to the skull cap thus forming the center part. Stitch the second piece over the first on the opposite side. The hair is now ready to braid, and to tie with ribbon bows.

Short Hair

This wig (*Fig. 16*) is used a great deal when a girl is going to enact a boy's role. Make a skull cap following the step-by-step directions at the end of this chapter. Cut a strip of crepe paper across the grain 1-inch wide.[1] Cut it along one edge into fine fringe.[2] Beginning at the lower edge of the cap, sew or paste the fringe on using two layers at once. Overlap the rows and when the wig is complete, ruff the fringe up with the palm of your hand to give it a softer look. Cut short rows of fringe where necessary to fit over the ears.

APRONS AND CAPES

THERE ARE MANY times when an entire fancy costume is not needed. A peasant apron or a rose petal cape, for example, over a simple frock will turn the trick.

Such quick-trick costumes are easily made of crepe paper. Many of them can be made for a few pennies, and in a few minutes.

For church suppers, teen-age kitchen parties, and lawn "socials," handkerchief size aprons, gathered to billowing fullness of vari-colored papers, are festive attention getters. The bottom edges can be left plain or they can be fluted,[3] fringed,[2] finger scalloped,[17] or trimmed with bands of many colors stitched on, or with a very frou-frou edge trim of twisted petals.[18]

Two aprons, one over each hip, worn over a long dress, caught up and puffed will give a panier effect quickly and inexpensively.

To make aprons, cut the necessary amount of paper remembering that the grain must run from waist to apron's edge. If you want to make an apron over 20-inches long, you must piece [21] your paper. Gather the top and sew it to a ribbon band.

Capes can be made just like aprons. For a witch's cape with a high collar, gather the crepe 6-inches from the top and sew a ribbon over the stitches allowing long ends for tying. To make a rose petal cape, shape pink crepe paper into rose petals as described for the child's rose costume in Chapter V. Gather the base of the petals and stitch a ribbon over the gathers leaving ends long enough to tie.

See General Direction 1, *p.* 223; 2, *p.* 223; 3, *p.* 224; 17, *p.* 232; 18, *p.* 232; 21, *p.* 234

HAWAIIAN LEIS

As COLORFUL AS flowers themselves, much more lasting, and as easy-as-pie to make, paper leis (*Fig. 17*) are a gay discovery. Even children can make them. For gaiety give one to each guest at a picnic, a lawn party, or a South Sea dancing party.

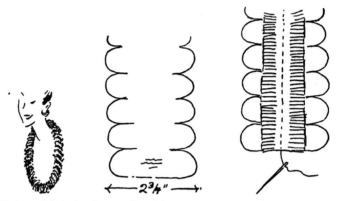

(Left to right) Fig. 17 Hawaiian leis of paper; Fig. 18 Diagram for petal shapes for leis; Fig. 19 Stitching two strips together to form leis.

Materials Needed to Make One:

1 fold crepe paper red
1 fold crepe paper yellow
Needle, soft cotton or silkateen thread

NOTE: *Any two bright colors of crepe paper may be used.*

Step 1. From wrapping paper make a pattern (*Fig. 18*).[12] Cut a strip [1] of red crepe about 2¾-inches wide.

Step 2. Open up the strip of crepe. Refold it to about eight thicknesses, pin your pattern in place with the grain of the crepe running in the same direction as the three lines on the diagram, then cut the entire strip into petal shapes, moving the pattern along the strip as you cut. If the last few petals don't jibe perfectly with the pattern, it won't matter.

Step 3. From yellow crepe cut a strip 1¼-inches wide right through the entire fold. Open the strip up and stretch it slightly. Refold it to about eight thicknesses, pin it here and there to hold the layers together, then slash it into fine fringe along each edge leaving a path about ¼-inch wide along the center uncut.

See **General Direction 12,** *p.* **229; 1,** *p.* **223**

[148]

Step 4. Place the fringed crepe paper on top of the petal strip and sew the two together down the center length with a long running stitch using a thread 40-inches long (*Fig. 19*). Gather the strips tightly.

Twist the strips around and around and you will see them taking on the characteristic shape of the famous lei. Join the ends of the thread by knotting them. Sew ribbons for tying to each end.

CREPE PAPER HATS

THE SKULL CAP is the basis of most crepe paper hats no matter how dissimilar they may appear when finished. Because crepe paper can be stretched and cupped, widely varying styles of hats can be arrived at from the basic skull cap. As an interesting and quick experiment, make several doll size skull caps and see how you can stretch the edge of one to make a sombrero, how you can dent in the top of another to make an overseas cap, how you can fold under the edge of one and then stretch its edge to make a beret, how you can tie the top of an extra deep one to make a dunce cap. And that is just a beginning!

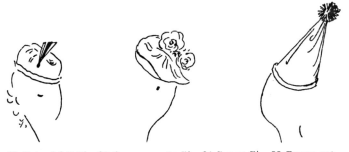

(Left to right) Fig. 20 Overseas cap; Fig. 21 Beret; Fig. 22 Dunce cap.

Skull caps that are used as a basis for wigs and that are, therefore, completely covered when finished, may be made as described below, but with knitted cotton underwear, a stocking top, or other two-way stretch material substituting for the crepe paper.

This is the easiest way to make a skull cap.

Step 1. Cut a strip[1] of crepe paper 10-inches wide, and long enough to reach around the head without overlapping. The grain of the crepe runs up and down with the 10-inch width. The average head size, by the way, is 22½-inches.

See General Direction 1, *p.* 223

[149]

Step 2. On the sewing machine, stitch the two 10-inch ends together making a seam of about ¼-inch (*Fig. 23*).

Step 3. Gather the top (about 2-inches from the edge) tightly with needle and thread. Secure the thread.

Step 4. Tie the top right over the gathers tightly with spool wire (*Fig. 24*).[6]

Step 5. Turn the lower edge up or under to make the cap the desired depth. The edge may be fluted.[3] (*Fig. 25* and *26*).

(Left to right) Fig. 23 Seam a strip to make a skull cap; Fig. 24 Tie the top of the skull cap with wire; Fig. 25 Skull cap with lower edge turned under; Fig. 26 Skull cap with lower edge turned up.

Note these choices of ways to proceed:

A. You can join the two ends with paste instead of with needle and thread. Paste is frequently used for dolls' hats.

B. You may skip gathering the top with needle and thread. If you do, simply gather it with your fingers and tie it with spool wire.

C. You may make the cap double. Many experienced handlers of crepe paper always make caps double. To do it, use the entire 20-inch width of the crepe paper, fold it through the center across the grain and proceed with Step 2.

D. You may seam and tie the top of the hat on the wrong side, then turn it right side out. The dull side of the crepe is the right side.

E. When the cap is done, you may cut off any surplus crepe above the spool wire. Spread out and flatten what's left.

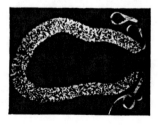

Here is an Hawaiian lei made of crepe paper. It's fluffy, it's colorful—it will never wilt. Directions for making it are on Page 148.

See General Direction 6, *p.* 226; 3, *p.* 224

CHAPTER VII

Beautifying Halls and Homes for Dances and Parties

BEFORE TRIMMING ANY *hall for a dance, bazaar, party or other function, make inquiries about fire prevention laws. What are your local ordinances? Your state laws? Some states prohibit the use of any but fireproofed materials; other rulings may affect your plans.*

So you're going to have a party! If it's a home affair, perhaps you're looking for some quick, A B C simple ways to strike a note of gay frivolity. Maybe it's a club get-to-gether and you're looking for a gay, easy and inexpensive trim for the club rooms. Or, perhaps, it's the Year's Party of Parties, the big Charity Ball, the High School Prom. You want a plan that will turn the old gym into a glamourous night spot—from pumpkin to Golden Coach via the magic wand of your decorating scheme.

Here then you will find some gay trims for impromptu affairs; trims-with-a-theme, especially useful for clubs, schools, etc., and elaborate decorations for important formal parties.

GAY TRIMS FOR IMPROMPTU AFFAIRS

HERE ARE FOUR A B C simple ways to give your home that "we're having a party" look. They're spark plugs to ignite the party spirit in your guests!

5-Minute Trim

This is the old mardi-gras stuff of crepe paper streamers. As a rule you can buy them, 2-inches in width, in a variety of giddy colors. When you can't, you can make your own quick as a wink.[30]

Twist them and they'll spiral like fat corkscrews. Drape them over the sofa (*Fig. 1*); loop them in swags along the stairway's balustrade (*Fig. 2*); catch them on the chandelier and stretch them to the four corners of the room; festoon them over open door-ways and windows (*Fig. 3*); Scotch tape will hold them in place. In spots where Scotch tape won't do the trick, spool wire can sometimes be used to tie them down. Thumb tacks are perfect when permissible.

See General Direction 30, *p.* 239

[151]

Fig. 1 (Upper left)
Drape over a sofa.

Fig. 2 (Lower left)
Streamers along a stair-
way.

Fig. 3 (Upper right)
Streamers over a win-
dow.

5-Minute Trim Plus

In the sketches illustrating the 5-Minute Trim, you've noted the addition of ribbon bows, sprigs of holly and jack-o'-lanterns.

Here are some additional ideas for quick, inexpensive trims to strike holiday and other keynotes.

Patriotic: Red, white, and blue streamers, plus ready-made cardboard cut-out shields, clusters of flags, stars, the American Eagle or other patriotic symbols.

St. Patrick's Day: Green streamers plus gold cut-out shamrocks.

Community Money-Raising Rally: Streamers plus posters bearing numerals representing the amount to be raised.

Lodge Installation of Officers: Streamers in the lodge colors plus cardboard cut-outs of the lodge's insignia or initials.

Any holiday decoration or any organization's color scheme can be carried out easily and effectively with the 5-Minute Trim *Plus* cut-outs.

Miracle-Whip-Up Trim

This flowering vine that you can whip up without paste, wire or patterns, is a bit of sleight-of-hand that is more fun and lots easier than blowing bubbles. It can be used for simple decorations or the most elaborate of trims. It can be used to trim a Christmas tree, to festoon booths at bazaars or to decorate walls or ceilings for a dance.

Step 1. Cut a strip [1] of crepe paper about 1-inch wide. Now open it up.

Step 2. Cut another strip in a different color, about 2-inches wide. Open this strip up, and cut off a series of 2-inch lengths. No need to use a ruler. You don't have to be accurate.

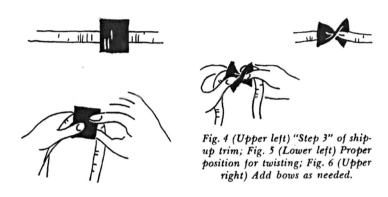

Fig. 4 (Upper left) "Step 3" of ship-up trim; Fig. 5 (Lower left) Proper position for twisting; Fig. 6 (Upper right) Add bows as needed.

Step 3. Lay a 2-inch square on top the 1-inch strip with the grain of the crepe running from top to bottom of the square (*Fig. 4*).

Step 4. With your fingers in the position sketched (*Fig. 5*), twist the strips together, twisting away from you with one hand and toward you with the other. This twisting will fasten the square to the strip and at the same time give an ornamental, scrolled effect.

Step 5. Add other squares in the same way, spacing them to suit your taste (*Fig. 6*).

With this simple process you can get the following effects:

Floral Vines. Cut the squares in various flower colors. Before opening up the 1-inch wide strip, flute [3] the sides slightly. This can make a luxuriant floral trim for an elaborately decorated dance hall.

Christmas tree decorations. Use any two Christmas colors, red on green for example. Cut the long strip only ½-inch wide; the squares about 1-inch. You will get a quick, inexpensive and easy-to-handle material to drape, in popcorn and cranberry strand fashion over a Christmas tree.

Circus gay. Use various colored vivid squares like turquoise, cerise and bright, light green on yellow and you will get a giddy carnival effect.

May Pole. Try this trim using spring flower colors on a pale green

See General Direction 1, *p.* 223; 3, *p.* 224

[153]

strip for spring festivals, pageants and other springtime events.

Lighting. A hoop draped with crepe paper fringe (*Fig. 7*) and festooned with the Miracle-Whip-Up can be used to cover a lamp or light fixture.

Balcony or Railing. Figure 8 shows a gym balcony which has been covered with plain yellow crepe paper stretched and tacked in place, decorated with festoons of Miracle-Whip-Up.

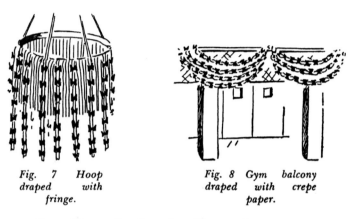

Fig. 7 Hoop draped with fringe.

Fig. 8 Gym balcony draped with crepe paper.

How to Dim Your Lights for Home Dances

Pretty, quick-to-make, and guaranteed to reduce electric lights to moonbeam faintness, is a big four-sided bag (*Fig. 9*), each side made of two layers of crepe paper. Stitch the four sides together on the sewing machine. To hold the bag open at the top, paste spool or No. 9 or 10 wire around the upper inside edge. Wrap it first with a strip of crepe paper [7] so that it will stick to the bag when pasted.

Fig. 9 Dim the lights with a heart shaped bag.

See General Direction 7, *p.* 227

[154]

Tie the bag to the chandelier with ribbons. Decorate it with cutouts and bows, if you wish. See Chapter IV for tying bows.

Note sketch of bag. Two sides are red, two white, St. Valentine's color scheme. The same heart shapes can be cut from orange crepe and decorated with black cut-outs to make Jack-O'-Lantern faces. Do them up in green and white for St. Patrick's Day, decorating the white sides with green shamrocks, the green sides with gold ones; use the school colors for a loyal school gang party.

TRIMS-WITH-A-THEME

IF YOU WANT your party trim to declare, not only "hi-ho, we're having a party," but also what sort of a party you're having, the theme of your party, consider these ways of getting over the idea.

A Basic Recipe

You want to say: "This is a Washington's Birthday Dance"; or, "This is a St. Patrick's Shindig," or, "This is a Rally to Raise Funds to Build a Swimming Pool for our High School," or—simply—this is a "Moonlight and Roses Party."

Fig. 10 Washington's Birthday trim.

Fig. 11 Moonlight and roses trim.

No matter what idea you want to get over for your party, an easy way to do it, is to make cardboard posters for the idea or theme, place them around the room, and link them together with either the 5-Minute Trim or the Miracle-Whip-Up Trim or straight streamers of crepe paper—note the Washington's Birthday Trim (*Fig. 10*).

In place of the posters you can use other spot motifs. In the Moonlight and Roses Theme (*Fig. 11*), the roses are the Quick Fake Roses; [26] the moon and stars are pale gold and silver foil cut-outs pasted to cardboard.

See General Direction 26, *p.* 237

Holiday Themes in Jig-Time

Although the following trim is for a St. Valentine's Day home party, you can easily transpose it to Halloween, St. Patrick's Day or Christmas. "A Calendar of Party Trims" in the last section of this chapter will prove helpful.

It's your turn to entertain the gang and it's just around the corner from February 14th, so you decide at practically the last minute to make it a Valentine Party. You dash out and buy or make red and white crepe paper streamers [30] and red heart cut-outs. Also get some large white paper lace doilies and some gold paper.

Fig. 12 Mantelpiece trim.

Clear off the mantelpiece, leaving only the mirror or large picture in place. Make a huge Valentine from a big red heart, edging it with the paper lace doilies cut in half and pasted on the underside. Paste a gold paper arrow on the heart and letter a sentimental message in white show card paint—something like "Be Mine" or "My True Love," etc. Fasten the heart to the mirror using gummed Scotch tape (*Fig. 12*). If you have some low candleholders, use one on each end of the mantel with tall white candles. Tie small red hearts at the base of the candles with spool wire and/or ribbons. Fasten a cluster of red and white crepe paper streamers at the top of the mirror with Scotch tape and drape streamers to each side.

Make a similar heart Valentine to cover every picture in the room, or to hang on the walls between draped crepe paper streamers (*Fig. 13*).

You do not have time to make complete window trims, so you call on the faithful crepe paper streamers to help you again. Twist red, and white streamers right over the draperies. Pin them on, they have no

See General Direction 30, *p.* 239

[156]

Fig. 13 Streamer wall trim hung between hearts.

weight and will not mark the fabric. Add more Valentines as fake tie-backs (*Fig. 14*).

Side Lights? Make heart shades to cover them (*Fig. 15*).

This theme may be elaborated upon by using your imagination to decorate a room to the best advantage.

Fig. 14 (Left) Valentine window trim with tie backs. Fig. 15 (Above) Heart shades for side lights.

Want something frilly? Make yards and yards of Floral Vine, as described earlier in this chapter, and festoon it around the ceiling lights and door-ways.

Popular Songs for Themes

Dance halls can often be decorated effectively by using a popular song as inspiration. To illustrate how it may be done we have taken one imaginary but typical song, and are describing below decorations that might be built around it. Picture-making phrases from the song, "a starlight dream," "beneath a garden wall," "when roses grow" give us fine pegs on which to drape our decorations. In similar fashion, lovely decorations can be developed around the great number of popular songs with appealing themes. Change the colors and suit the motifs to the song's title and to picture-making phrases in the lyric. Any popular or semi-classical song with a romantic theme and using such words as June, love and moonlight can be used to provide an exciting atmosphere for any dance.

To decorate for a Starlight dance, here are some suggestions. Use a stone garden wall with garlands of flowers, great quantities of silver stars and sky blue, light and dark, crepe fringe, and streamers.

A garden wall can be made of ordinary tan wrapping paper. Mark it off into large field stone shapes with black and brown crayons. Around the base of the walls, wherever they fit, put sections of the paper wall. Over it drape flower garlands. Make these of crepe paper evergreens.[25] Pin, paste or staple wild roses to them. The wild roses can be made, and very effectively, in this extremely simple way. Simply cut circles of tissue paper from as many shades of pink to red tissue paper as you can lay hands upon. Don't try to cut them regularly. Simply snip them up as carelessly as can be. If they only remotely resemble circles, they'll be all right. In size they can range from silver-dollar to tea-cookie. In fastening them to the garlands, don't pin them on to make them lie flat. Fold them so that they will stand out from the garland. Give your wild roses a varied look, by pasting to the center of some of the large pale pink circles, smaller bright pink circles, and vice versa. In making these garlands of wild roses, it is advisable to make about a yard, twist, and try it to see if you have the roses spaced to please you, before completing all of the garlands. A stapling machine is excellent for attaching the tissue flowers to the garlands. No paste needed! Everything done in one quick punch operation!

High above the walls arrange sweeping clusters of silver stars in various sizes cut from silver foil paper—a Milky Way effect. Between each cluster of stars place a flower garland.

To decorate the ceiling lights, use pale blue crepe paper, curly fringe over white curly fringe.[20] See "Light Trims" in this chapter. Around the top of each fringed shade arrange another garland of wild roses.

To make a decorative ceiling, festoon streamers of crepe paper [29] in two shades of blue from the lights to the walls. Twist the streamers to give that pretty spiral look. See "Ceilings" which follow in this chapter.

On pillars and posts, use the flower garlands again cutting narrow ones. Spiral them around and around. See "Pillars and Posts" which follow in this chapter.

Cover the windows with draperies of curly, pale blue crepe paper fringe tied back with garlands of flowers.

Outline the doors with a double row of the flower garlands. Scotch tape will hold some of the decorations in place. Spool wire can be used to tie the garlands to the light trims. Thumb tacks, of course, are ideal

See General Direction 25, *p.* 237; 20, *p.* 234; 29, *p.* 239

wherever they will not mar woodwork and walls.

Hoops, My Dear!

A barren old hall or gym can be given a quick beauty treatment by using a series of hoops. Decorated and placed around the walls with streamers connecting them, they make a gay decoration to carry a theme. The hoops can be trimmed in advance and put up in record time by a number of workers. Here are a few suggestions:

For Winter, Christmas: Curly white crepe paper fringe [20] with large red poinsettias pinned around the hoop (*Fig. 16*).

For Spring: Hoop wrapped and festooned with pale green crepe paper and encircled with apple blossoms (*Fig. 17*).

For Fall: Bright orange or yellow crepe paper fringe on the hoop and a wreath of cut-out autumn leaves made from bright colors of construction paper or mat stock (*Fig. 18*).

The hoops may be used in any one, or all, of the following ways:

(Left to right) Fig. 16 Christmas wall trim on a hoop; Fig. 17 Spring wall trim on a hoop; Fig. 18 Autumn wall trim on a hoop.

Walls: Decorate the hoops and place them at intervals flat against the walls with twisted streamers draped between them.

Windows: Hang a small decorated hoop in each window.

Lights: Encircle each with two hoops of different sizes. Pin fringe to the inner hoop and the Miracle-Whip-Up, for example, to the outer.

Additional suggestions are offered in "A Calendar of Party Trims" in the last section of this chapter. This calendar givs an appropriate theme for every month of the year and color schemes to fit each occasion.

See General Direction 20, *p.* 234

Flying Banners

An easy way to strike a decorative note is with the use of crepe paper banners. They are especially appropriate for trims suggested by such names as "Mediaeval," "Old Spain" and "Sports Carnival." They are also useful in covering unsightly wall spaces and unused windows.

Fig. 19 Wall banner with colored borders.

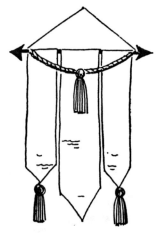

Fig. 20 Wall banner with tassels.

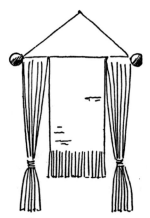

Fig. 21 Wall banner with fringe.

The top of the banner is a dowel stick or an old broom stick. The knobs and arrows on the ends of the stick are usually two cardboard cutout shapes fastened together, with the stick between them, with glue or

[160]

staples. There is no limit to the style and shape of the banners. The illustrations show just three of many:

Figure 19 shows three strips of crepe paper in one color with wide borders of a contrasting color. Tassels [24] and rope [28] are made of crepe paper.

Figure 20 shows three panels of crepe paper, pointed at the ends, two outside panels trimmed with tassels. The cord and tassel hung across the top of the banner are made of crepe paper.

Figure 21 shows how a center panel of crepe paper is trimmed with crepe paper fringe,[20] two side panels are fringe tied at the bottom with crepe paper to form a tassel end.

ELABORATE DECORATIONS FOR FORMAL PARTIES

To MAKE THE old gym lush with glamor, each architectural feature from ceiling to doorways must be given a beauty treatment. Here are some suggestions for complete transformations.

Plan the Trim in Advance

Step 1. Choose a suitable theme for the occasion. Select your color scheme. A Calendar of Party Trims is given in the last section of this chapter.

Step 2. Examine the hall to be trimmed; take all measurements; check on the use of tacks, gummed tape, wire—etc.

Step 3. Make rough plans of each wall as a flat unit showing doors, windows, posts, balcony. Make rough sketches of the lights.

Step 4. In pencil, mark on your plans the location of each wall unit of decorations. A few well planned units of decoration, repeated to give continuity to the decorations will be easier to handle and more effective than a great variety of units. They'll be quicker, too, for you can prepare several units at one time by cutting through several thicknesses of paper around one pattern.

Lights

Crepe paper fringed shade (*Fig. 22*). Use a wooden or wire hoop, cardboard reinforced with wire (for a hoop) or laths fastened to make a square. Make the hoop or square foundation considerably larger than the light fixture, so that the paper will not touch the bulb. If you cannot purchase a wire hoop, make one by piecing together several No. 7 or 15 wires and wrapping them with narrow strips of crepe paper.[7] Wrap them before you bend them to shape.

Cut curly fringe.[20] Pin two or three thicknesses of fringe over the

---

See General Direction 24, *p.* 236; 28, *p.* 238; 20, *p.* 234; 7, *p.* 227; 20, *p.* 234

edge of the foundation. Decorate the top with flowers or holidays symbols such as hearts, shamrocks, bells and shields. When this is done attach four pieces of wire evenly spaced to the top of the hoop or square for fastening the shade to the light fixture.

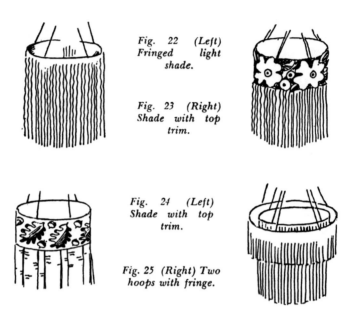

Fig. 22 (Left) Fringed light shade.

Fig. 23 (Right) Shade with top trim.

Fig. 24 (Left) Shade with top trim.

Fig. 25 (Right) Two hoops with fringe.

Figures 23 and 24 show two styles of top trim.

Figure 25 shows the use of two hoops with the fringe on the inside hoop twice as long as the fringe on the outside hoop.

Figure 26 shows a square foundation with the fringe cut in scallops. The square shade lends itself particularly well to the use of decorative emblems—note the shield and stars for a patriotic trim.

Figure 27 shows the use of narrow crepe paper streamers pinned around a wire hoop. The decorative value of this simple trim lies in the use of color; red and white for Valentine's Day; orange and black for Halloween; school or club colors.

Figure 28 shows a wire hoop with paneled fringe crepe paper.[27] This type of light decoration may be trimmed with cut-outs such as bells, stars, pumpkins, flowers. A strip of a contrasting color may also be pinned to each solid panel.

Figure 29 shows how to make a central light appear larger. Long

See **General Direction** 27, *p.* 238

sticks are fastened across the top of the hoop to form extensions to which fringe or streamers are pinned.

Fig. 26 Shade with square foundation.

Fig. 27 Streamer pinned around a hoop.

Fig. 28 Paneled fringe trimmed with cut-outs.

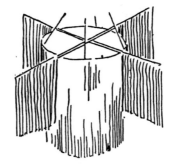

Fig. 29 Shade for making light appear larger.

Balconies

Figure 30 shows crepe paper fishnet.[22] This is for a nautical trim. The life belts sketched are cardboard cut-outs.

Figure 31 shows crepe paper banners in two colors. The smaller topping the larger gives the border effect. The colored paper letters are pasted on. Apply the paste to the letters.

Figure 32 shows crepe paper drapery. It is made by stretching the full fold of the crepe paper and gathering it at the ends to fasten in swag fashion to the balcony. Several folds of paper are used for bulk in each section.

Figure 33 shows a formal garland of draped crepe paper strapped

See General Direction 22, *p.* 234

with a contrasting color of crepe paper cut across the grain and finished with a heavy crepe paper rope [28] and tassels.[24]

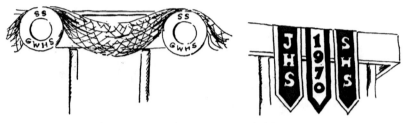

Fig. 30 (Left) Balcony draped with fishnet.
Fig. 31 (Right) Banners over a balcony.

Fig. 32 (Left) Balcony drapery; Fig. 33
(Right) Formal garland of crepe paper.

Posts

For a very simple trim use crepe paper streamers to carry out the color scheme. For more elaborate decorations a post may become a tree

(Left to right) Fig. 34 Wooden arm on post; Fig. 35 Vertical streamer on post; Fig. 36 Bands with holly cut-outs.

See General Direction 28, p. 238; 24, p. 236

in bloom, a palm tree or a statuesque tassel. You can change the shape and style of a post by adding branches or wooden "arms" at the top. Scotch tape is helpful in fastening decorations when pins and tacks cannot be used. Wire wound around posts can also be used to anchor decorations in place.

Figure 34 shows how to add a wooden arm to the top of a post. Crepe paper streamers or fringe can be festooned to this.

Figure 35 shows the use of vertical streamers and symbols.

Figure 36 shows bands around a post with holly cut-outs. Flowers, fruits, or autumn leaves can be used for other seasons of the year.

Fig. 37 (Left) Posts with cut-out flowers.

Fig. 38 (Right) Streamers and fake roses wound barber pole fashion.

Figure 37 shows a post with cut-out flowers concentrated at the lower level.

Figure 38 shows Quick Fake Roses [26] made into a spray, and streamers [29]—wound barber pole fashion around a post.

Ceilings

Many halls and gymnasiums have ugly ceilings, with unsightly beams or pipes which should be covered or at least disguised. To cover a ceiling completely is not only a long and tedious job but if you are working with a modest budget it is also apt to be a prohibitive one. However, there are several comparatively easy and inexpensive ways to make ceilings prettily festive.

Method One: Use lights as centers of attraction and radiate crepe paper streamers or fringe from light to light and from light to walls. Picture wire or heavy twine fastened to small screw eyes at stated intervals around the top of the wall, or at the level at which you wish to create the false ceiling, will serve as a foundation to which the

See General Direction 26, *p. 237; 29, p. 239*

streamers may be fastened. If you cannot put screw eyes around a picture moulding or at a chosen height on the wall it's best to forget a ceiling decoration and concentrate on lights, windows, etc.

Method Two: Place screw eyes along all four walls at a point slightly higher than the ceiling height you've decided on. String wires or twine from screw to screw and fasten the wire ends firmly.

What you use on your wires will depend of course on your decorative theme. For a circus or nautical trim you may want to use bright crepe paper pennants; for a Christmas Party, exaggerated holly made of large green paper leaves and bright red paper berries balloon size; for a winter or Snow Ball party, white crepe paper cut into icicles.

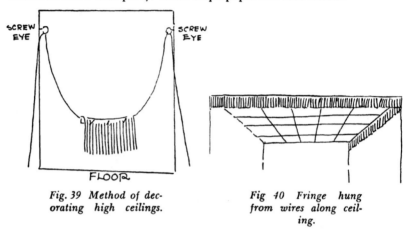

Fig. 39 Method of decorating high ceilings.

Fig 40 Fringe hung from wires along ceiling.

When a ceiling is too high to be decorated from ladders, the device illustrated in Figure 39 can be used. Fringe, pennants or other paper trims can be pinned to the wire by workers standing on the floor. When the decorations are in place the wire ends can be pulled, thus hoisting the trim.

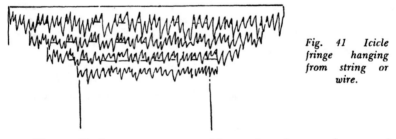

Fig. 41 Icicle fringe hanging from string or wire.

Figure 40 shows crepe paper fringe pinned to a wire or twine strung across a ceiling. For clarity in the sketch the fringe is not shown on all the wires.

Figure 41 shows crepe paper cut into an "icicle" edge and pinned to wire or twine.

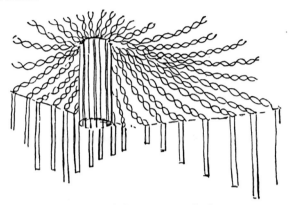

Fig. 42 Streamers attached to center light and draped to each side of the room.

Figure 42 shows streamers attached to a center light and draped to each side of the room where they are fastened by pins to a wire strung around the top of the walls.

Windows

Crepe paper makes festive and inexpensive draperies. Made in the background color or a combination of colors to carry out the color

Fig. 43 (Left) Crepe paper streamers with a twisted streamer valance.

Fig. 44 (Right) Decorated valance and fringe drapes.

scheme, they often add a great deal to a room's appearance. Windows can also be disguised and made an integral part of the decoration. One way of doing this is with criss-crossed crepe paper streamers making a lattice work to which cut-out paper flowers are pinned. These flowers can be cut from tissue paper as explained for making the garlands under "Popular Songs for Themes" earlier in this chapter.

Crepe paper draperies can be stitched, just like cloth, on the sewing machine.

Figure 43 shows a window made colorful with crepe paper streamers. The valance has twisted streamers, the sides straight-hanging ones.

Figure 44 shows a window with a plain crepe paper valance decorated with cut-outs and curly fringe used as side drapes.

Figure 45 shows a window entirely covered by crepe paper fishnet [22] to which large cut-out paper flowers have been pinned.

Fig. 45 Window covered with paper fishnet and cut-out flowers.

Doors

It is clever to bring door-ways into the decorating picture. Figure 46 shows a door with a simple crepe paper swag across the top and

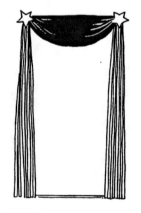

Fig. 46 (Left)

Fig. 47 (Right)

See General Direction 22, *p.* 234

streamers at the sides. Stars, shamrocks, hearts, and other symbolic cut-outs can be used for fake tie-backs. Figure 47 shows clown heads and balloons decorating a doorway draped with streamers.[29]

Archways

If your hall contains an open stairway, you may want to decorate the bottom of the stairway with an arch. This may be done by building a rounded arch from heavy wire, or lightweight laths which are supple enough to bend in a curve. Fasten the laths or wires to the posts (often they can be tied with wire) and wind both posts and laths several times with folded strips [1] of crepe paper, to give thickness and a foundation to which you can pin the rest of the decoration.

Fig. 48 (Left) Archway decorated for Christmas.

Fig. 49 (Right) Archway with spring or summer trim.

Figure 48 shows twisted streamers, cut-out trees and a Christmas bell.

Figure 49 shows a similar arch treated for a spring or summer trim with large cut-out flowers and crepe paper fringe. The posts are wrapped with strips of crepe paper in soft green to harmonize with the flowers.

A CALENDAR OF PARTY TRIMS

No MATTER WHAT sort of a function you're planning decorations for, the following January-through-December suggestions may prove helpful. Use them in connection with the trims described previously in this chapter. Two of the trims that may prove especially useful are the 5 Minute Trim—Plus, and Hoops, My Dear!

Color schemes may be carried out with whatever decorative mate-

---

See General Direction 29, *p.* 239; 1, *p.* 223

rials you're using, crepe paper, flowers, plants, balloons, ribbons, lanterns, construction paper, etc.

January Theme:
Winter or "Snow Ball"
Units: Cut-out snow men, or icicles, penguins, polar bears, skaters, skiers
Colors: white, green, blue

February Theme:
A Valentine Dance
Units: Cupids, hearts, arrows, or large valentines
Colors: red, pink, white, gold

March Theme:
St. Patrick
Units: Cut-out clay pipes, shamrocks or high hats, the Blarney Castle, harps
Colors: green, white, gold

April Theme:
Easter
Units: Bunnies, chicks, ducks, flowers, birds, eggs (Choose one or two)
Colors: all delicate shades, pink, green, orchid, yellow, pale blue

May Theme:
Maypole Dance
Units: Maypoles with crepe paper streamers—flowers and birds. (Maypoles can be silhouetted wall decorations)
Colors: delicate shades as listed for April
or

May Theme:
Child Health Day Program
Units: The official flower is the daisy. Use it with poster-type figures of children
Colors: yellow, white and green

June Theme:
Rose
Units: Use oversize roses.[26] A lattice on the windows with

See **General Direction 26**, *p.* 237

[170]

climbing roses is effective.

Colors: rose, pink, light and dark green

July Theme:

Patriotic (This is also appropriate for February)

Units: Flags, shields, stars, Lincoln or Washington silhouttes in black. Cherries or hatchets in cardboard cut-outs for February 22.

Colors: red, white and blue

August Theme:

Nautical

Units: Sailboats, gulls, waves, pennants. (Fishnet [22] is helpful)

Colors: blues, greens and white

September Theme:

Autumn or Indian Summer

Units: Cut-out autumn leaves, Indian figures and symbols, such as the moon, sun, and stars.

Colors: bright fall shades, blue, red, yellow, green, gold, orange, purple

October Theme:

Halloween

Units: Cats, witches, pumpkin faces, owls, bats and ghosts

Colors: black and orange with touches of sharp green

November Theme:

Harvest

Units: Hay Stacks made of crepe paper (these can be flat cut-outs or 3 dimensional for corners, door-ways and other floor spots) pumpkins, turkeys or fruit, autumn leaves, horn of plenty, harvest moon, flying geese.

Colors: brown, yellow, orange, green

December Theme:

Christmas

Units: Santa Claus or holly wreaths, candy canes, bells, stars, etc.

Colors: red, green and white, gold and silver

See General Direction 22, *p.* 234

CHAPTER VIII

Glamorizing Banquet Tables

As A RULE without too many exceptions it's pleasant to decorate the front skirt of the speakers' table, but only the tops of the other tables.

Three layouts for tables are shown. There are, of course, many other arrangements. Figure 1 shows the tables forming an A for America, for a Patriotic Banquet. Figure 2 shows a C shape facing a full-size portrait

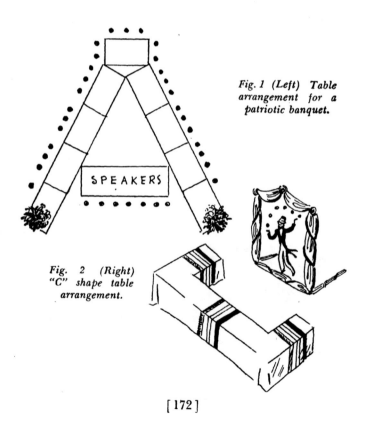

Fig. 1 (Left) Table arrangement for a patriotic banquet.

Fig. 2 (Right) "C" shape table arrangement.

frame, back of which entertainers can put on their acts. Figure 3 shows tables arranged around a fake campfire, an appropriate arrangement for Boy Scouts and Campfire Girls.

Fig. 3 Table arrangement for outdoor clubs.

Table Covers

It's easy to carry out any color scheme by resorting to that practical material which comes in so many colors—crepe paper. As it is only 20-inches wide, it is often necessary to seam it.[21]

If you're carrying out a two-color effect, use the lighter color for the cloth, the darker for the trim as a rule.

Trims

The easiest way to strike your color scheme and at the same time to get a trim, is with the use of crepe paper streamers.[30] These can be laid on in a variety of patterns as shown by Figure 4.

Fig. 4 Patterns for streamer trim.

See General Direction 21, *p.* 234; 30, *p.* 239

[173]

The easiest way to carry out a holiday trim is to use place mat symbols of the occasion: Hearts for St. Valentine's Day, and bells for Christmas, all cut from crepe paper.

Crepe paper streamers and candles (*Fig. 5*) will complete the decorative units. Do not use paper place mats, as the color is not fast, over table linen.

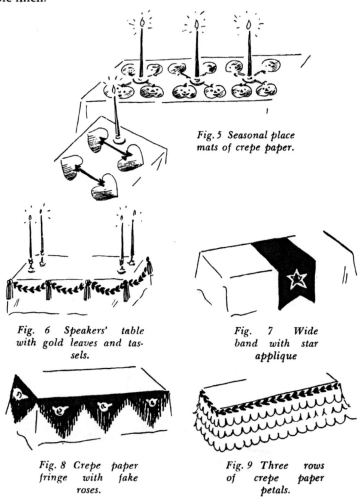

Fig. 5 *Seasonal place mats of crepe paper.*

Fig. 6 *Speakers' table with gold leaves and tassels.*

Fig. 7 *Wide band with star applique*

Fig. 8 *Crepe paper fringe with fake roses.*

Fig. 9 *Three rows of crepe paper petals.*

Speakers' Table

For some occasions a rather elaborate front skirt is desired for the speakers' table. Figures 6, 7, 8 and 9 show some attractive trims.

CHAPTER IX

Eye-Catching Booths for Fairs and Bazaars

Is IT TIME to consider ways and means of raising money for the church, school or club? If you're asking people to buy tickets for a fair, see to it that you give them a treat for their money—an evening that is really gay and festive, plenty of entertainment, and a carnival atmosphere for buying the wares that devoted workers have contributed.

The first problem is to have a definite idea for your fair. Here are a few suggestions which are described in detail later in this chapter.

A State Fair with a booth for a number of different states.

A Calendar Fair with a booth for each month.

A Family Af-Fair with a booth for each member of the family from Grandma to Little Brother.

A Cairo Street Fair.

How to Build Booths

You can use plain rectangular or round tables, planks resting on saw-horses, or you can have uprights added to plain tables. The value of

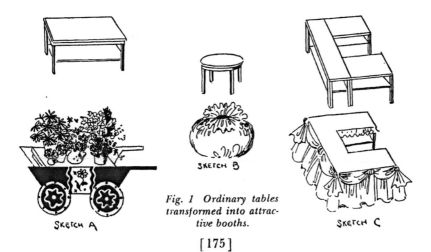

SKETCH A

SKETCH B

SKETCH C

Fig. 1 Ordinary tables transformed into attractive booths.

uprights is that they are attention getters over the heads of the milling crowds. Figure 1 shows plain tables and how they have been simply converted. Figure 2 shows rather elaborate carpentry. These booths, of course, lend themselves to a great variety of decorative effects. Note the sketches for a Calendar Fair booth.

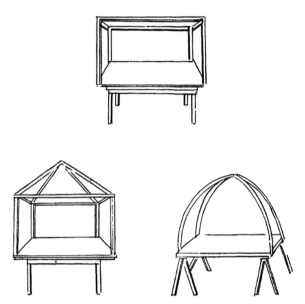

Fig. 2 Three basic ways to build booths.

How to Decorate Booths

Crepe paper is the most widely used material for booth decoration. This is because, without doubt, it is inexpensive, comes in a wide variety of colors and is capable of performing many tricks. The tricks you will use in decorating booths are in Chapter XV. Here are some of the tricks that are of especial use to the booth decorator: How to Cut Crepe Paper Fringe,[20] How to Make Crepe Paper Streamers,[30] How to Make Tassels,[24] How to Make Crepe Paper Rope,[28] How to Make Quick Fake Roses,[26] The Miracle-Whip-Up Trim, Chapter VII, How to Make Fishnet,[22] How to Make Twisted Petal Edges,[18] How to Make Fringed Pom-

See General Direction 20, *p.* 234; 30, *p.* 239; 24, *p.* 236; 28, *p.* 238; 26, *p.* 237; 22, *p.* 234; 18, *p.* 232

pons.[23] How to Gather Crepe Paper.[15] How to Join Two Widths.[21] How to Drape Crepe Paper.[33] All of these will prove helpful.

A State Fair Bazaar

First decide on the number of booths you wish to have. Then give each booth the name of a state choosing the state best suited to the merchandise to be sold. Here are some ideas:

Georgia. This could be a Coke bar where cola drinks are served by a southern belle in hoop skirts. Peaches and leaves cut from paper and colored sketchily with crayons could be pasted here and there to a simple green crepe paper foundation.

Alabama. Cotton goods—aprons, handkerchiefs and crocheted novelties—could be sold at this booth which might display impressionistic cotton blossoms (balls of cotton and green paper leaves) against a green or yellow crepe paper skirt background.

Nebraska. Home-made preserves and pickles might be sold from a booth masquerading as a red barn by salespeople costumed as farmers. The stage version of the farmer costume, overalls and straw hats, would get over the idea.

California. Flowers sold from a booth sporting a gay striped awning, which can be made of paper, should stamp the booth as California.

Florida. Fruits, marmalades, honey might be offered for sale at a booth flanked by paper palm trees in silhouette.

Similar ideas can be developed around merchandise tied up with other states.

A Calendar Fair

The thumb nail sketches and brief notations will start you on your way with this fair. Except when otherwise specified, all the materials mentioned in the notations are crepe paper.

January (*Fig. 3*). Skirt, light green fringe [20] with white streamers [29] caught up with a silver bell, a foil cut-out . . . posts wrapped [7] in light green . . . icicles cut from white across top . . . table top, white.

February (*Fig. 4*). Skirt, pale pink spotted with gold foil hearts . . . uprights wrapped in white . . . pink fringe [20] on top centered by large gold foil heart . . . table top, pink.

March (*Fig. 5*). Skirt, bright green fringe [20] with white overskirt punctuated with a big cardboard shamrock . . . top draperies,[33] white . . . table top, green.

See General Direction 23, *p.* 235; 15, *p.* 231; 21, *p.* 234; 33, *p.* 240; 20, *p.* 234; 29, *p.* 239; 7, *p.* 227

April (*Fig. 6*). Skirt, pastel colored fringe,[20] several colors, cut in scallops . . . posts, table top, and overhead draperies,[33] yellow . . . spot decorations, construction paper cut-outs of Easter eggs and bunnies.

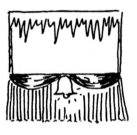

Fig. 3 January theme.

Fig. 4 February theme

Fig. 5 March theme.

Fig. 6 April theme.

May (*Fig. 7*). Representing a Maypole, this booth has one center upright wrapped [7] in yellow . . . streamers,[20] hanging from pole top, many colors . . . pole top encircled with artificial flowers . . . skirt, alternating scalloped flounces of yellow and white.

June (*Fig. 8*). Skirt, pink with dark green points to suggest a rose and its calyx . . . posts, wrapped [7] in green . . . green streamers [20] swagged from top to sides and caught back with over-size pink roses.

July (*Fig. 9*). Skirt, red, white and blue fringe [20]. . . posts and table top, white . . . top drapery,[33] red, white and blue caught up ʼn center with a cardboard cut-out shield . . . smaller shields strung across top.

See General Direction 20, *p.* 234; 33, *p.* 240; 7, *p.* 227; 29, *p.* 239

August (*Fig. 10*). Skirt, two shades of blue cut into wave-like scallops . . . posts, dark blue . . . white fishnet [22] draped at the side . . . skirt front decorated with large silver fish, a silver foil cut-out.

Fig. 7 *May theme.*

Fig. 8 *June theme*

Fig. 9 *July theme.*

Fig. 10 August theme.

September (*Fig. 11*). Skirt, orange points over brown . . . posts, wrapped [7] in yellow . . . uprights decorated with autumn leaves cut from construction paper in rich autumnal colors.

October (*Fig. 12*). Skirt, orange fringe . . . posts,[7] wrapped in black . . . table top, black . . . top and side decorated with cardboard Jack-O'-Lanterns and green vines.

November (Fig. *13*). Skirt, alternating ruffles of yellow and green . . . posts and table top pale yellow . . . haystacks, formed with straight crepe paper fringe,[20] yellow, tan, green . . . real pumpkins.

December (*Fig. 14*). Skirt, tiers of red ruffles . . . posts, wrapped [7] with

See General Direction 22, *p.* 234; 7, *p.* 227; 20, *p.* 234

green . . . green cardboard trees trimmed with paper cut-out ornaments, bells, stars, candy sticks, bows, and candles.

Fig. 11 September theme.

Fig. 12 October theme.

Fig. 13 November theme.

Fig. 14 December theme.

A Family Af-Fair

Mother's Booth. This might be devised to represent a pantry, with shelves displaying Mother's jams, jellies, cakes and bread. The shelves could be edged with paper lace doilies; the skirt of the booth might be clear yellow crepe paper with red ruffles.

Father's Booth. Tobacco pouches, bill folds, book marks, men's knitted mufflers and similar masculine paraphernalia might be sold from a booth suggestive of a ranch. The sides of the booth could be covered with brown wrapping paper. A thatched roof could be made from crepe paper fringe,[20] cut with the grain, in a mixture of yellow, green, brown and orange. The booth could be decorated with paper cut-outs of steer heads, wagon wheels, lariats and sombreros.

See General Direction 20, *p.* 234

[180]

Grandmother's Booth. Aprons could be sold from a booth decorated in lavender and "old-lace." Crepe paper could be used for a lavender skirt of three ruffles each edged with paper-lace.

Sister's Booth. Candy is sister's choice. Her booth might have a skirt of pink ruffled crepe paper. At each corner there could be giant peppermint stick posts. Someone good at carpentry and painting would have to put these up.

Little Brother's Booth. This could be the ever profitable grab bag. To make one around an inverted circular table see Figure 1. The bag is made of crepe paper. Widths are joined with Scotch tape, gathered and thumb-tacked to the bottom of the table. Tissue paper is padded between the bag and the legs, which have ordinary wrapping paper pasted to them forming four walls. The top of the bag is gathered.

A Cairo Street Fair

The booths can be ordinary tables with mosque-shaped cardboard fronts painted with poster paints in brightly colored simple geometric designs. Booth tops might be covered with cotton Persian prints or with plain deep colored cotton.

The usual fair merchandise can be sold, but if possible, one booth, at least, should offer some Oriental novelties: inexpensive costume jewelry, incense and brass ware.

All attendants should be in costume, the women in long dresses with bright colored sashes. Head bands or veils covering the lower part of their faces, dangling bracelets, necklaces, and flowers in their hair will be sufficiently suggestive of the East. Men can wear plain white blouses with dark trousers, wide sashes and fez turbans.

Oriental rugs over chairs, couches, balconies, oriental music, girls in costume with trays suspended by ribbons around their necks selling candies, nuts, and cakes will create more atmosphere.

Character dolls of crepe paper raffia are sold at many church and school fairs. Basic directions for making "Raffia" dolls are given on Page 217.

[181]

CHAPTER X

Rainy Day Fun for Children

IT'S RAINING AND the children get squeamish. They're tired of their toys; they want something NEW to do! Set them busy with scraps of paper, cardboard, and some paste.

And soon—instead of; "RAIN, RAIN GO AWAY!" It will be; "RAIN, RAIN STAY TO-DAY!"

Here is some rain-day fun for children. All of the materials needed should be at hand in the home.

Milk Bottle Book Mark

Any child who likes books, and is starting to read, will enjoy making this simple and practical book mark (*Fig. 1*).

Fig. 1 Milk bottle book mark.

Materials Needed to Make One:

2 milk bottle covers
1 piece of ribbon
Crayons
Glue

Draw pictures with crayons on one side of each of the milk bottle covers. Apply glue to the back of one of the covers. Lay ribbon on it, then press the other glued cover over it. Set between two books to dry.

Paper Cup Baskets

These little cups (*Fig. 2*) are fun to make. They can be used for favors at a child's party to hold little candy mints.

Fig. 2 Paper cup basket.

Materials Needed to Make One:
　1 small paper cup
　2 wire shanks
　A magazine with colored ads
　Paste

Punch a small hole on either side of the paper cup. Cut a strip of colored paper for the handle about 1 by 6-inches. Punch small holes at both ends. Fasten the handle to the cup with the wire shanks. Cut out pieces of colored paper from the magazine. Paste them to the cup to make a picture.

Fan-Fun

Little girls playing house will love to make these colorful fans *(Fig. 3)*.

Fig. 3 Paper fan.

Materials Needed to Make One:
　Medium-weight cardboard
　Ribbons or colored string
　Crayons or a magazine with colored ads
　Paste

Using a small plate as a guide, draw a circle on cardboard. Cut the cardboard leaving a square piece for the handle. Cut two holes in the handle and tie a ribbon or colored string through them. Cut out colored sections or colored pictures from the magazine and paste them on for decorations.

[183]

Sewing Cards

This "busy time" project (*Fig. 4*) provides entertainment for little tots who are not too dexterous with their hands.

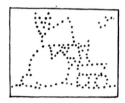

Fig. 4 Sewing card.

Materials Needed to Make One:

Lightweight cardboard about 4 by 6-inches
Crayons
Darning needle
Colored thread, embroidery floss or string

Draw and color any simple object such as an animal, tree or flower. Punch holes with a large darning needle around the outline and use bright-colored thread for sewing in and out the holes.

Sewing Picture Books

If enough pieces of cardboard are used, all ages of "small fry" can paste up and bind their own books (*Fig. 5*).

Fig. 5 Picture book.

Materials Needed to Make One:

Lightweight cardboard
Colored pictures from magazines
Darning needle and colored yarn
Crayons
Paste and scissors

Paste or draw pictures on several pieces of cardboard. Punch holes on the left side of each card with the darning needle. Place the cards one on top of the other and sew them together with yarn and the darning needle. The children will be delighted with the results.

Paper Clock

The making of this paper clock (*Fig. 6*) helps children to tell time at an early age.

Fig. 6 Paper clock.

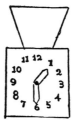

Materials Needed to Make One:

Cardboard or construction paper
Crayons
1 wire shank

Letter numbers in a circle on the cardboard. Cut out two pieces of cardboard, one for the large and one for the small hand. Punch a hole at the ends of both and in the center of the square.

Cut out a V-shaped piece for the stand and punch a hole in it. Place the three pieces together and fasten with a wire shank.

Indian Tent

Making a whole village of Indian tents (*Fig. 7*) is a day's project which children of all ages will enjoy.

Fig. 7 Indian tent.

Materials Needed to Make One:

Brown wrapping paper
Crayons, seals or a magazine with colored ads
Paste

Cut a circle about 4-inches in diameter from brown wrapping paper. Then cut it in half and make a V-shaped opening on the circle side for doorway. Decorate the tent with crayon drawings, or paste on stars, moons or circle seals. Cut the shapes from colored sections of magazines.

[185]

Fold one straight edge of this semi-circle over the other and paste the edges together.

Indian Canoe

These authentic looking canoes (*Fig. 8*) make a decorative addition to a village of Indian tents.

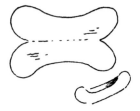

Fig. 8 *Indian canoe.*

Materials Needed to Make One:
Brown wrapping paper
Toothpicks
Crayons, brown or black
Paste

Cut a piece of brown wrapping paper about 4 by 6-inches. Fold it as indicated by the dotted line in the sketch and round off the corners of the open edges for bow and stern. Paste the ends together. Punch holes for the seats with a needle, and put toothpick seats through them. Decorate by streaking with crayon.

Paper-Box Cradle

Any child will delight in making this simple cradle (*Fig. 9*).

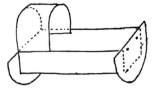

Fig. 9 *Paper box cradle.*

Materials Needed to Make One:
Shoe Box or Cracker Box
Heavy white paper and cardboard
Paste

Color the sides of the box with paint or crayon. Cut a circle from the cardboard with a diameter a little larger than the ends of the box. Cut this in half for the two ends of the cradle. Paste them to the box or fasten them to it with two wire shanks.

Cut a strip of heavy white paper and form a hood. Paste it to the cradle.

Paper Bead Necklace

This necklace (*Fig. 10*) is a pleasant old standby and one which children always get enthusiastic about.

Fig. 10 (Left); Fig. 11 (Right) Triangular strips for beads.

Materials Needed to Make One:
Brightly-colored pages from a magazine
Toothpicks
Elastic cord
Shellac
Paste, scissors

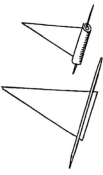

Step 1. From a magazine page, cut triangular strips of various sizes. Long strips will make thick beads, wide strips will make wider beads. Make one bead of each size to determine which one you will use.

Step 2. Place strips, colored side down, and roll tightly around toothpick.

Fig. 12 Strips being rolled on toothpicks.

Fig. 13 (Left) End of strip is pasted down; Fig. 14 (Right) Toothpick is removed when shellac is dry.

Step 3. Paste down the end.

Step 4. Apply shellac over the paper bead. When it is dry, remove the toothpick.

Step 5. String the dry beads on elastic cord. Any number of combinations may be achieved as one large bead, then two smaller ones, or a graduation of sizes tapering down from the middle.

CHAPTER XI

Paper Crafts that Cater to the Imagination

THIS CHAPTER DESCRIBES five projects that are particularly generous to the imagination, giving it plenty of scope. Teachers of arts and crafts will find them interesting assignments—practical, too, from a financial point-of-view as the cost of the materials needed is negligible.

You Can Make Christmas Tree Balls and Other Decorative Articles With This Unusual Paper Craft

Lightweight, colorful and non-breakable, Christmas tree balls of paper are a delight to make *(Fig. 1)*. For school art classes they are an excellent assignment. Planning the cut-out decorations can be a designing problem as simple or as advanced as the class is qualified to undertake. The cost is only a few cents each when a quanity are made.

Fig. 1 Christmas tree balls of paper.

The balls are formed by a method closely related to making papier maché. Decorations are cut from colored papers and pasted.

Materials Needed to Make One:

1 ball for a foundation mould (tennis, baseball, or a Christmas tree
ball)
Waxed paper (enough to wrap the ball in)
Crepe paper for forming the ball
Scraps of colored papers or foils for the decorations
String to form the loop for hanging the ball
Paste, scissors and a razor blade

(Left to right) Fig. 2 Foundation ball wrapped with waxed
paper; Fig.3 Ball wound bandage fashion; Fig. 4 The crepe
paper shell cut in two; Fig. 5 The ball wrapped to a smooth
finish.

Step 1. Wrap your foundation ball in waxed paper (*Fig. 2*). Simply crush
the paper around the ball as you would if you were wrapping an
apple in paper. The purpose of the waxed paper is to prevent the
crepe paper and paste from sticking to the ball.

Step 2. Across the grain of your crepe paper, cut a strip ½-inch wide.[1]
Open the strip up.

Step 3. Wind the ball with the strip stretching the crepe paper and pasting it down as you do the winding. Wind and wind in bandage
fashion (*Fig. 3*) until the ball is smoothly covered with a thin shell.
About five complete wrappings will do the trick. The paste and
paper creates what amounts to papier maché. Let the ball dry. This
will take some time. If the ball making is an art class assignment,
the balls had best dry until the next meeting of the class. In the
meantime, if the period is not over, the students can work on
planning their own individual decorations.

Step 4. With a razor blade, cut the crepe paper shell in two (*Fig. 4*).

Step 5. Paste or sew a ribbon loop to the center top of one half.

Step 6. Paste the two halves together.

Step 7. Rewrap the ball several times with the crepe paper strips stretching them completely and pasting them down to give a smooth
neat surface (*Fig. 5*).

See General Direction 1, *p.* 223

Step 8. To the ball, paste cut-outs of foil or bright colored papers.

Over-size Easter eggs, so popular for gift boxes, can be made in the same way. In similar fashion small occasional boxes for dressing or end tables can be designed and made.

Papier maché boxes are imported to this country from the Far East, India producing them with amazingly elaborate hand painted decorations. From Mexico come similar boxes with striking Indian designs; France has sent us papier maché boxes of great beauty. Many of hers have become museum pieces. Whether handcrafts are your hobby, or part of your work, you can find almost limitless inspiration for creating lovely designs and useful articles from this simplified form of papier maché work.

How to Model Cork Head Bottle Stops

Nearly all little children like to make mud pies. There's proof that most of us were born with a pleasure sense that responds to using our hands for modelling!

It isn't necessary to have marble or even clay to enjoy modelling. Crepe paper reduced to a dough-like consistency with paste makes an excellent modelling material for certain projects.

Roll up your sleeves, and try this as your initiation. It is, by the way, an excellent art class project. Each student following the dictates of his imagination can create his own characters, for this is a head-and-face modelling spree.

Students of the Evander Childs High School in New York working under Miss Laura Cowell, instructor, modelled these little figures of crepe paper using the same general procedure described for modelling cork heads in this chapter.

[190]

Materials Needed to Make One:
1 cork 2-inches high
1 nail about the same height
Crepe paper skin color
Crepe paper yellow, brown or carrot for the hair
Crepe paper blue or brown for the eyes
Crepe paper red for the mouth
Paste, "white" shellac, clear lacquer or colorless liquid nail polish

(Left to right) Fig. 6 Step 1 in modelling cork heads; Fig. 7 Step 2 in modelling cork heads; Fig. 8 Step 3 in modelling cork heads; Fig. 9 Step 4 in modelling cork heads.

Step 1. Pierce the cork with the nail *(Fig. 6)*.

Step 2. Stretch and crumple a square of skin colored crepe paper. Cover one side with paste. Wad it up and crush it around the nail *(Fig. 7)*. If this isn't the right size, paste on more paper. The head, at this stage, doesn't have to be smooth.

Step 3. Add another paste-moistened wad of crepe paper to give the back of the head its shape *(Fig. 8)*.

Step 4. Cut a strip of crepe paper, skin color, ⅜-inches wide.[1] Wind this around the head firmly, stretching it and pasting it down here and there. As you proceed with the winding, shape the head with your fingers. Its moist paper will respond readily *(Fig. 9)*.

Step 5. To the forehead, chin and cheeks paste on small paste-moisted wads of crepe paper stretching them before you dampen them with paste. Add a similar bit of paste-soft paper for the nose. Shape it *(Fig. 10)*.

Step 6. Cut a square of crepe paper, skin color, large enough to drape over the entire head. Stretch it until no crinkles are left. Cover the head with paste and lay the stretched-thin paper over it blending it in as smoothly with the face contour as possible *(Fig. 11)*. Add more paste if necessary. Take up any slack in the paper in the back which will probably be covered later by hair or a hat.

See General Direction 1, *p.* 223

Step 7. Add the features. These, too, can be bits of paste-wet crepe paper. Put them in place with tweezers or the points of your scissors, for the wet crepe colors will bleed onto the skin color. If you prefer, you can make the mouth of a bit of red crepe paper twist.[19]

Step 8. Make the hair. This can be crepe paper raffia, see the beginning of Chapter XII, pasted in place. It can be crushed [16] or fringed [20] crepe paper—also pasted on. See how to make wigs in Chapter VI. The hair, no matter what kind, can be pasted directly to the skull.

NOTE: *As the entire head is to be lacquered or shellacked when dry, do not attempt to make curls that hang away from the head. The wig should have a "modelled to the head" look.*

(Left to right) Fig. 10 Step 5 in modelling cork heads; Fig. 11 Step 6 in modelling cork heads; Fig. 12 Mammy modelled of crepe paper; Fig. 13 Dutch girl modelled of crepe paper.

Step 9. Allow the head to dry thoroughly. Depending upon the climate this will be an over-night or longer process. When it is completely dry, brush it with clear lacquer or shellac that has been exposed to the air long enough to thicken it. Alcohol in very thin shellac will make the colors run.

The sketches show a Story-Book Mammy (*Fig. 12*) and a Dutch Girl (*Fig. 13*). The former has brown ski · and a red and white kerchief; the latter has blond braids and wide blue eyes.

Historical characters such as Cleopatra, Queen Elizabeth; characters in fiction, Cyrano with his long nose, Old King Cole with his jolly round face and crown; or national characters, a Spanish Toreador, a Chinese Emperor, all of these and countless others, offer possibilities.

Paint with Paper Appliqués

These paper plates (*Fig. 14* and *15*) can be wiped clean with a damp cloth. They have been decorated with paper cut-outs then covered with several coats of clear lacquer which has given them a pottery-like look.

See General Direction 19, *p.* 233; 16, *p.* 232; 20, *p.* 234

Paper plates so decorated can be used for serving popcorn, nuts, candies, or they can be used as decorative spots to hang on kitchen or breakfast room walls.

Fig 14 (Left); Fig. 15 (Right) These show two paper plates with appliqués.

School or camp craft classes will find making these plates an interesting assignment—and an inexpensive one, a matter of a few cents for each student.

Other things that can be decorated in the same way with paper appliqués are: paper bowls, boxes, scrap book covers, desk sets. The sketches (*Fig. 16, 17, 18* and *19*) show four boxes.

 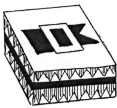

Fig. 16 (Left) A glove box. Fig. 17 (Right) A belt box. Both boxes have been decorated with paper appliqués.

Fig. 18 Paper appliqués on a trinket box.

Fig 19 Paper appliqués decorating a box for sweaters.

[193]

Materials Needed:
    Paper plates or boxes, for foundations
    Colored papers for cut-outs
    Paste, clear lacquer or shellac, scissors

NOTE: *If no store in your community carries solid colored papers you can use crepe paper. Directions for using it follow.*

Fig. 20 (Left); Fig. 21 (Right) These show two different designs for paper appliqués for paper plates.

Step 1. Cut out the various units that are to make your design. Sketches for two designs are given in Figures 20 and 21, for a 10-inch plate. Enlarge them to the necessary dimensions. Use vivid and sharply contrasting colors.

Step 2. Apply library paste to the back of each unit and lay it carefully in place. Do not smudge the paste beyond the cut-out.
    Before following Step 2, you may wish to trace your design lightly onto the plate. The outlines will help you in placing each unit.

Step 3. Allow the design to dry completely, then cover the plate back and front with a quick coat of clear lacquer or shellac. When that has dried, apply another, and then—allowing time for drying, another.

CAUTION: *Because shellac contains alcohol it causes some types of dyes to run. Test your papers before you apply the shellac. As a rule even if the colors do bleed, trouble can be avoided by brushing on the first coat quickly and lightly and by using a shellac that has been thickened a bit by exposure to air.*

To use crepe paper for appliqués. From wrapping paper cut patterns of each part of your design. Cut squares of white note paper a little larger than your patterns. Cover the note paper with a thin smooth coat of paste. Over it place a square of crepe paper. Rub it with the grain of the crepe. Place a pattern over the pasted square and cut around it. Cut out each part of the design and paste it in place on the plate. Then proceed to shellac or lacquer the plates as described above.

CHAPTER XII

Projects for Camp, School, Church, Settlement Houses and Hospital Groups

HERE ARE SOME simple and inexpensive crafts for children selected with the needs in mind of teachers in schools, camps, and settlement houses. Many of the items can be made from things that are usually thrown away; those that can't, call for easy-to-find and inexpensive materials. Although the items are simple, each one can give the child's imagination a chance to create in its own way.

Crepe paper raffia, an inexpensive and easy-to-prepare material is used to make many articles.

CREPE PAPER RAFFIA—A HANDCRAFT DISCOVERY

A SLEIGHT OF HAND trick which is mere child's play for simplicity converts paper into a raffia or yarn-like material of countless uses.

It can be used to weave baskets, bowls and place mats. It can be braided, woven, or crocheted to make pocket-books, belts, costume jewelry, bracelets, necklaces and lapel gadgets for sports or play clothes. It can be used to wrap around old bottles, cans, boxes to transform useless throw-aways into pretty and useful articles. It can be used to crochet hats. It even makes rugs of surprising sturdiness.

Crepe paper raffia has the advantage of being inexpensive and available. There is probably not a town in America that doesn't, during normal times, have at its stationery, drug, department or chain store a supply of colorful crepe paper.

Crepe paper raffia has the disadvantage of not being washable. Many of the articles made from it are lacquered or shellacked for a finish; others can be shaken to free them from dust. Hats, bags, and belts made of deep colors will bleed if exposed to rain, snow or perspiration.

How to make it. By far the easiest, though not the only, way to make crepe paper raffia is to use a little gadget developed for that purpose, called a Crepe Paper Twister. Priced at about a dime, it's a little block of wood with two tunnels running through it. A substitute for the Twister is a button, a button with a hole in it.

[195]

To make the raffia with either the Twister or the button, cut your crepe paper into narrow strips [1] across the grain. Instructions in this book specify the exact width when it's important. One inch is average, but strips can be as narrow as ½-inch or as wide as 2-inches.

After cutting your strip, open it up. Twist one end to a fine point and thread it through a hole in the Twister or button. Then stretching the strip slightly on one side of the Twister or button, pull it through the other twisting it as you pull (*Fig. 1*).

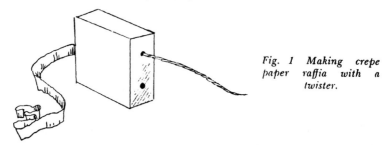

Fig. 1 *Making crepe paper raffia with a twister.*

If you use a button, you may have to try several before you get one with a hole the right size. It must be small enough to crush the paper but not so small as to break it.

After a very little practice you can pull yards and yards in no time at all if you use a Twister; a button slows matters up.

Tie Rack

This tie holder (*Fig. 2*) is so simple that a child can make it easily.

Fig. 2 *Tie rack of crepe paper raffia.*

See General Direction 1, *p.* 223

Materials Needed:

 Crepe paper

 1 piece of corrugated cardboard (about 8¼ x 1½-inches)

 3 rubber jar rings, paste

Make crepe paper raffia as described on the preceding pages. Cut the strips for it ½-inch wide. Wrap the cardboard strip around and around with it, pasting down the "raffia" ends. Wrap the rings around and around, too. Then, wrap them to the cardboard with separate strips of raffia, and finally—wrap the three rings together in the same way. From the raffia, braid a handle and with a raffia strand tie it in place.

(Left to right) Fig. 3 Ivy bowl of crepe paper raffia; Fig. 4 Tea caddy of crepe paper raffia; Fig. 5 Hot pot holder.

Ivy Bowl

 An ivy bowl like the one sketched (*Fig. 3*) is very decorative.

Materials Needed:

 1 old glass jar (some marmalade jars are perfect)

 1 fold crepe paper light tan for foundation

 1 fold crepe paper orange for stripes and braided handle

 1 fold crepe paper blue for stripes and braided handle

 1 fold crepe paper green for stripes and braided handle

 Glue, paste, shellac

 First coat the bottom of the jar with shellac. Allow it to dry, make crepe paper raffia, cutting your strips of paper about 1-inch wide for the jar, 2-inches for the handle.

 Begin at the bottom of the jar and glue down the end of the crepe paper raffia. Then wrap the "raffia" around and around and up the sides to the beginning of the border. As you wind the strands push them

[197]

snugly against the previous row. It isn't necessary to glue the strands continuously except on the bottom. Put it on here and there, just enough to hold to the sides of the jar. Use the glue sparingly. When it's necessary to join strands of raffia, paste is better than glue.

Make the braided handle with loose ends forming tassels. Glue it lightly in place before winding the top of the jar. (A 50-50 combination of glue and paste can be used in place of the pure glue.)

Tea Caddy

Useful and decorative when covered with brilliant colored crepe paper raffia, the tea caddy (*Fig. 4*) is a good gift item.

Materials Needed:
1 tin can
Wooden button and nail for the knob
1 fold crepe paper light tan for foundation
1 fold crepe paper orange for stripes and braided handle
1 fold crepe paper blue for stripes and braided handle
1 fold crepe paper green for stripes and braided handle
Glue, paste, shellac

NOTE: *If a wooden button and nail are difficult to get, a handle can be made of a loop of braided crepe paper raffia with its ends poked through a hole in the top and glued to the underside. A circle of cardboard can be pasted over them for a neat finish.*

Coat the bottom of the can, and the top and bottom of the lid with shellac and then proceed as in making the ivy bowl. Make the crepe paper tassel [24] using crepe paper raffia in place of fringe.

Pocket for Hot Pot Holders

Primary grade children can turn these (*Fig. 5*) out and feel quite a sense of achievement when their work is done. A present to take home from school!

Materials Needed:
2 paper plates, about 8-inches across
Paper napkins, with colored printed designs
3 small wire shank fasteners
A gummed cloth suspension ring or a piece of ribbon for hanging the pocket
Paste, glue or rubber cement

Cut one plate in two. Cover it and the whole plate with a light smooth coat of paste and lay the paper napkins in place. Trim the edges.

See General Direction 24, *p.* 236

Fasten the two plates together with the wire shanks, glue, or rubber cement and put the suspension ring on the back. If you use rubber cement, apply it to both edges and let it dry slightly before pressing them together.

If the design on your paper napkins lends itself to the effect, don't cut the paper plate straight through the center, but cut it to the napkin's design. Note Figure 5. Don't worry if the napkins wrinkle a little. It's because they have a crepe texture that they are good to use.

Crepe Paper Raffia Bracelet

Teen age youngsters will enjoy making this (*Fig. 6*) as the bracelet is attractive to wear. Gay colors for the weaving and a neutral color, like tan, for the foundation work up effectively.

Fig. 6 Crepe pa-
per raffia bracelet.

Materials Needed to Make One:
> Crepe paper, four or five colors
> Light weight cardboard (correspondence folders are the right weight)
> No. 7 or 15 wire
> Paste, "white" shellac (optional), gummed paper tape

Step 1. Following the pattern shown in Figure 7, cut two pieces of light weight cardboard. Strengthen one with the two pieces of wire attaching them to it with patches of gummed paper tape (*Fig. 8*).

Step 2. Place the other cardboard piece over it, and hold the two together with gummed paper pasted over the cardboard (*Fig. 9*).

Step 3. Make crepe paper raffia in several colors. See first part of this chapter. Suggested color scheme: Light tan raffia for the background; green, blue, orange and dark brown for the pattern of broken stripes.

Step 4. Cut one 8-inch length of each of the colors chosen for the stripes

[199]

and paste them to one end, backside, of the bracelet (*Fig. 10*).

Step 5. Wind a strip of crepe paper raffia, the color selected for the background, around and around the bracelet. As you wind, weave your strip over the colored strips and then under them, so that they show part of the time and are concealed part of the time. Paste the crepe paper raffia down when you start winding it, use a little now and again to help keep the vertical winding upright, and as you approach the opposite end of the bracelet, paste the colored strips down on the backside. The colored strips can be worked out to form a regular pattern or they can be hidden and, then revealed, in willy-nilly fashion. The only caution is not to leave them exposed for more than about ½-inch lengths. They are apt to catch and be torn when worn if greater lengths are exposed.

Step 6. When the bracelet is done, bend it to shape. If you wish, give it a quick light protective coat of shellac or clear lacquer. Don't brush the shellac in.

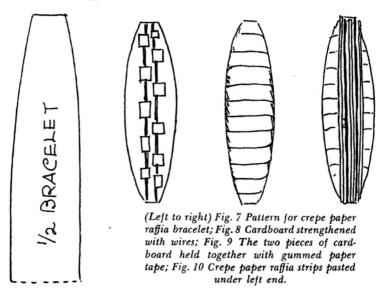

(*Left to right*) *Fig. 7 Pattern for crepe paper raffia bracelet; Fig. 8 Cardboard strengthened with wires; Fig. 9 The two pieces of cardboard held together with gummed paper tape; Fig. 10 Crepe paper raffia strips pasted under left end.*

Corrugated Cardboard Animals

Challenge to the imagination! What animals can a group of children create from 1-inch wide strips of corrugated cardboard? Figure 11 may start the creative ball a-rolling.

Materials Needed:

Corrugated cardboard (this must be smooth on one side, corrugated on the other, and light enough to bend easily.)

No. 9 or 10 wires (Picture wire could substitute.)
Crepe paper for tails, manes and winding
Paste, gummed paper tape

Shape each section of the animal from two strips of the corrugated cardboard, pasting the smooth sides together. If the cardboard needs to be extra stiff, as for a horse's back, gum tape two lengths of wire between the two strips.

Make some crepe paper raffia cutting the strips of paper a bit under 1-inch in width. For instructions for making the "raffia" see the first part of this chapter. Bind the two strips of corrugated cardboard. together by winding the "raffia" round and round in the furrows. This gives color to the designs. Make the tails, manes, etc. of the raffia, tying it on in bunches.

Fig. 11 Corrugated cardboard animals.

A Tray in Homespun Craft

The tray illustrated (*Fig. 12*) is just one of the many items that can be woven by a simplified process called Homespun Craft. It differs essentially from conventional basket weaving.

[201]

Unlike the latter, Homespun Craft is quick, easy, and most inexpensive. The items made from it do not, of course, have the life-time durability of those made in the old-as-Moses method employing reeds. What they lack in durability they make up in colorfulness, and ease of making.

The step-by-step directions below are for a circular tray. Following the same method you can make bowls, and boxes.

Fig. 12 A tray in homespun craft.

Materials Needed:

1 paper plate, 8-inches in diameter
Crepe paper, two or three colors
A "bobby" pin or long eyed needle
Paste, "white" shellac or clear lacquer

NOTE: *Suggested colors for crepe paper: (1) Straw color for background, orange and light green for stripes. (2) Turquoise blue for background, cerise and black for stripes. (3) Yellow for background, rust and bottle green for stripes.*

Step 1. Make crepe paper raffia in the colors you have selected. Follow the directions at the beginning of this chapter. Cut the strips 1-inch wide.

Step 2. Cut twenty-five V-shaped notches around the edge of your paper plate. Make them about ¼-inch deep (*Fig. 13*).

Step 3. To the middle of the plate (underside) paste the end of a strip of "raffia," the color chosen for your background. Wind the strip through the notches back and forth following the diagram given (*Fig. 14*).

Step 4. Thread the strip of "raffia" with which you've been winding, through a "bobby" pin or needle, then start weaving around the center over and under every spoke of your tray (*Fig. 15*).

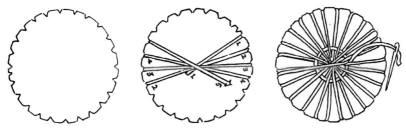

(Left to right) Fig. 13 "25"notches around edge of plate; Fig. 14 Winding crepe paper raffia through the notches; Fig. 15 The weaving started.

Step 5. If you wish, follow these proportions: Make your center circle, which is of the background color, say straw color, 2-inches in diameter. Then break your "raffia" strip and to it paste one of orange. Weave a few rows of orange. Break your "raffia" strip, and paste green to its end. Weave several rows of the green, edging them with a few rows of orange. Start weaving with your straw again continuing until your tray is about 5-inches in diameter, then weave several rows of green, a few of orange, several of green, and finally pick up the straw color. Paste it to the end of the green and continue weaving with it until you have reached the edge. Then break off and paste down the end of your weaving strip.

Step 6. Give the tray a coat of clear lacquer or shellac. When it has dried, lift it off the notches, and give both sides another coat. Two more coats, with a drying interval between them, will add to the sturdiness and lustre of your woven plate.

Woven Bowl in Clothesline Craft

This method, see Figure 16, is a moderately ambitious type of weaving, not the ABC simple process just described. As bowls and trays with geometric Indian patterns can be worked out it has considerable fascination for the person with feeling for handcraft work. The clothesline foundation gives the articles bulk and a look of some importance.

Materials Needed:
Clothesline rope

Crepe paper several colors
Tapestry needle
Paste, shellac

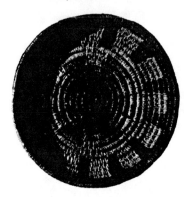

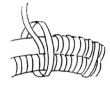
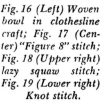

Fig. 16 (Left) Woven bowl in clothesline craft; Fig. 17 (Center) "Figure 8" stitch; Fig. 18 (Upper right) lazy squaw stitch; Fig. 19 (Lower right) Knot stitch.

Step 1. Prepare some crepe paper "raffia" from strips cut ¾-inches wide following the directions at the beginning of this chapter.

Step 2. Measure off enough rope to make the size bowl you want. An 8-inch shallow bowl requires about eight yards of clothesline; an oval tray about 7 by 10-inches requires 10-yards. Figure your rope generously for it can't be pieced.

Step 3. Thread your tapestry needle with a long strip of "raffia" in the color you want for the center of your bowl. Take the end of the threaded strip and with it wrap one end of the rope for about 2-inches. Roll the wrapped end into a tight circle for the center of the basket. Hold the circle in place with the "Figure 8" stitch (*Fig. 17*). Continue wrapping the rope and binding the rows together with the "Figure 8" stitch. After the circle is well started, you can introduce the following stitches and also additional colors. When you are using more than one color, carry the color not in use alongside the rope concealing it with the wrapping and binding stitches. Pick it up when you wish to bring in the color. *Lazy Squaw Stitch.* This is as easy as its name signifies. Wrap your raffia strip around and around the rope for about ½-inch, then bind it to the previous row with a long stitch around both (*Fig. 18*). *Knot Stitch.* This is illustrated by Figure 19.

When your basket is finished, cut the rope to a long thin point, and bind it with your winding stitches to the previous row. Paste the end of your "raffia" under the previous row.

Give the finished basket several coats of "white" shellac or clear lacquer allowing each coat to dry thoroughly before applying the next. Brush the shellac on quickly and lightly.

Serpentine Coasters

Here is a stunt with paper that deserves the popularity it has so long enjoyed, for the coasters made in the manner described emerge looking amazingly like a rough peasant pottery (*Fig. 20*).

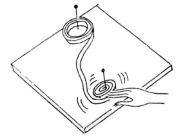

Fig. 20 Serpentine coaster.   *Fig. 21 Starting the coaster.*

Materials Needed:

1 package of serpentine paper, 20 rolls. (This is enough for four coasters about 3-inches in diameter.)

Paste, breadboard, pins, "white" shellac

Serpentine comes in assorted colors that combine to give an attractive striped pottery look.

Step 1. Select a color for the center. Put a roll of that color at one end of the breadboard and hold it there with a pin anchor (*Fig. 21*). Start unwinding the paper curling the end into a small, tight roll. Wind the paper around and around the center very tightly until you have a circle about 1-inch across.

Step 2. From this point on, instead of rolling the serpentine in your fingers, roll it from the original onto your roll as illustrated by Figure 21. Note that a pin through the center of the roll holds it in place and that you turn the roll around and around on the pin which acts as a pivot. As you roll to make the center brush the strip a bit now and then with paste. Don't use paste after the center is started firmly.

Step 3. When you are ready to introduce a new color, simply replace the first roll on the sketch with the new one. Join its end to your new roll with paste.

Step 4. When your roll is about 3-inches across, cut off your serpentine and paste it down.

Step 5. With the coaster flat on the breadboard, place your fingers on each side, and press it up gently all around the outside row to form a rim.

Step 6. Give the coaster at least six coats of shellac allowing each to dry thoroughly before applying the next.

[205]

CHAPTER XIII

Bright Touches for Your Home

MANY ATTRACTIVE AND useful articles can be made for the home from paper. Among them are lamp shades, waste baskets, rugs (yes!) and countless smaller things such as attractive picture frames, desk sets, glass jackets, wine carafes, cigarette boxes.

Aside from that, interesting decorative touches can be added to the home by the use of paper. Let's consider some of these first.

French Doors Go Modern

What to do with those French doors with their many panes of glass!

Make of each pane a little picture by backing it with a gay floral wall paper (*Fig. 1*).

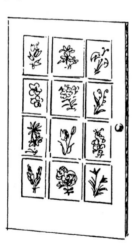 

Fig. 1 (Left) A French door modernized with wall paper. Fig. 2 (Right) A chest of drawers decorated with wall paper.

To do it: measure one pane. Make a cardboard pattern to fit it. From wall paper cut a shape to fit each pane. Cut another shape from metallic foil paper say, silver, gold, or copper. Back the wall paper with the metallic foil using wall paper paste preferably. With a small brush, border the edges of the wall paper side with wall paper paste. Press it against the pane. There's a pretty floral effect on one side, a smart metallic one on the other. The combination makes a pleasing pattern.

High Style for an Old Chest of Drawers

A hopelessly dowdy chest of drawers can emerge as an interior decorator's item with the help of a roll of wall paper (*Fig. 2*).

Materials Needed:
1 plain chest of drawers
Wooden or glass knobs
2 paint brushes
Wood filler
White undercoat and white enamel
Sandpaper
1 roll of wall paper, preferably in an all-over floral pattern
Wall paper paste, colorless lacquer

Step 1. Remove the handles from the chest. Fill the holes with wood filler. If it's old, give the chest a good scrub down. Sandpaper it, then carefully brush off all wood dust as tiny invisible particles of dust will give your chest a case of pimples.

Step 2. Apply the undercoat paint, and when it is completely dry, sandpaper it lightly. Brush off all dust particles and apply the enamel.

Step 3. Measure the drawers. Cut a paper pattern about 2-inches shorter and narrower than the drawers. Guided by it, cut wall paper panels for the drawers. Coat the back of each with wall paper paste and smooth them into place. There'll be a border of about 2-inches around each.

Step 4. Allow plenty of time for the wall paper to dry, then brush the surface with a clear colorless lacquer. If the wall paper you have used is a washable or water resistant one, the coat of lacquer can be skipped. However, as it gives a harder protective surface it is recommended even over washable papers. In buying the lacquer ask for a brand that will not affect colors in paper.

Step 5. Measure and mark the position for the knobs, and screw them into position.

BRIGHT WAYS WITH PICTURES

FROM INSIGNIFICANT PICTURES, post cards, greeting cards or old family-album portraits you can—with the tasteful use of paper—make smart little hangings. Mats chosen with an eye to the personality of the picture can turn a trick!

Flower Prints

You have a little flower print that you like? Get a framed picture.

A big one has more style. Remove the paper backing and small nails. Lift out the backing, mat and picture. Paint the frame with flat paint in a color that echoes one in the picture. Mount the flower print on a white paper lace doily. Mount it, in turn, on silver foil paper. Wall paper paste is excellent for an adhesive. Return it to the frame, reinserting the nails and backing. See Figure 3 for the final effect.

Fig. 3 (Above) Floral print mounted on paper doily.

Fig. 4 (Right) One-color sketch mounted on copper foil paper.

One-Color Sketch

A monotone sketch (*Fig. 4*) can take on a very modern look by mounting it as described above on an oversize copper foil mat, and by painting the frame in a sharp color, bottle green or royal blue, for example. Hung alone, such a sketch is apt to be insignificant; hung with a group, an effective composition results.

Fig. 5 Family album portrait mounted on wall paper.

Family Album Portrait

If the portrait is old and quaint, try to find an oval frame for it. Cover the mat with the wall paper in a small floral pattern, using library or wall paper paste or rubber cement. Form a very narrow border

[208]

around the photograph with fine crepe twist.[19] If the wall paper has rose colors in it, the twist might be in a deep plush red. Paste the twist in place and to the top paste a little bow.

Paste the oval portrait on the mat, and put it in the frame using the backing and nails that you removed from it (*Fig. 5*).

CREPE RAFFIA LAMP SHADES

ATTRACTIVE LAMP SHADES can be made easily and inexpensively from crepe paper raffia. Instructions for making it are given in Chapter XII. Waste baskets to match are described in this chapter.

Wrap Around

Easiest of all methods is the Wrap Around (*Fig. 6*). Note the shade. This model is in pink with crepe paper pompons in pink and rose attached to the bottom.

Fig. 6 Wrap around lamp shade.

Materials Needed to Make One:

    1 wire lamp shade frame
    2 folds crepe paper
    1 spool No. 1 wire
    Paste

Wrap [7] the rings forming the top and bottom of the shade with a narrow strip of pink crepe paper.

Prepare pink crepe paper raffia cutting your strips $3/4$-inch wide. Wrap them around and around the wire frame, pasting the raffia down at the beginning and at the end. When it is necessary to join two strips of raffia, do it with paste.

See General Direction 19, *p*. 233; 7, *p*. 227

When the lamp is completely covered, make pompons for the bottom in this way.

(Left to right) Fig. 7 Step 1 in making pompon; Fig. 8 Step 2 in making pompon; Fig. 9 Step 3 in making pompon.

Step 1. Cut a piece of cardboard 1-inch wide, about 3-inches long. Around it wrap your pink crepe raffia about thirty times (*Fig. 7*).

Step 2. Under the loops at one end, run a piece of spool wire about 4-inches long (*Fig. 8*).

Step 3. Tie the loops tightly by twisting the wire. Cut the loops at the other end (*Fig. 9*).

Step 4. Tighten the wire twist, for it must hold the raffia strips very securely. Fluff the pompon up, and if necessary trim the edges with your scissors. Tie the pompons to the edge of the shade with the ends of the spool wire. Twist, don't knot, the wires. Cut off any excess wire.

Wrap Around in Stripes

Child's play to make but smart in appearance, are Wrap Around shades made exactly like the shade just described but using three or more colors for perpendicular stripes (*Fig. 10*). Because of the great number of crepe paper colors to choose from, you can work out color schemes to tie in with slip-covers and draperies of almost any coloring.

Fig. 10 Lampshade and waste basket showing wrap around in stripes.

Three color schemes applicable to the striped pattern sketched are: pale yellow, rose, brown; light green, French blue, navy; gray, turquoise, American Beauty.

To finish the top and bottom of the Wrap Around shades, crepe paper braid can be pasted in place.

LOCKSTITCH CRAFT

HERE'S AN EGO-BUILDING craft. It looks complex enough to impress your friends, but actually it's so simple you hardly need your wits about you once you're started. In addition to that unquestionable virtue, its design and color possibilities are a challenge to even sluggish imaginations.

Three sketches are given which reveal the process, but hardly the simplicity, of this craft. Try the thing out for yourself with a little crepe paper raffia, and you will see at once how simple it is. Make a practice lesson of the Basic Instructions which follow.

Instructions are also given for making one lamp shade; hints on making a matching waste basket; and illustrations showing other items you can make via Lockstitch Craft.

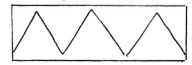 

Fig. 11 (Left) Step 2 in lockstitch craft; Fig. 12 (Right) Step 3 in lockstitch craft.

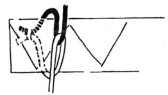 

Fig. 13 Step 3 continued.   *Fig. 14 Step 4 completed.*

Basic Instructions

Step 1. Make crepe paper raffia in two colors, cutting your strips (for a lamp shade) about ⅜-inches wide. See Chapter XII for making the "raffia."

Step 2. Tie the two colors together. Cut a piece of cardboard and with pencil mark in the zig-zag lines (*Fig. 11*).

Step 3. Place the knot on the back of the cardboard (*Fig. 12*). Bring one strip of raffia to the top, one to the bottom, and both around to the front. Loop one over the other (*Fig. 13*); and wind the colored strips right back where they came from; in the back, loop them over each other again (*Fig. 14*). Repeat and repeat.

In working out some effects you can draw your triangular designs on a cardboard base and work right over it. On some, as—for example— a lamp shade, that is impossible. You must let your eyes guide you. However, you can draw a section of your triangular motif on paper, and hold it in place from time to time as you need it.

[211]

Lockstitch Lamp Shade

This simple Lockstitch craft enables you to make smart lamp shades.

Fig. 15 Lockstitch lampshade; base and box.

Materials Needed to Make One:
　　2 folds crepe paper, two colors
　　Wire frame, paste

NOTE: *Three attractive color schemes for the crepe paper are forest green and white, powder blue and ruby, light yellow and orange.*

　　Wrap [7] the rings forming the top and bottom of the shade with a narrow strip of crepe paper.

　　Cover the frame with the Lockstitch as described under Basic Instructions. This section appears on the preceding page.

See General Direction 7, *p.* 227

Each triangle in the shade illustrated (*Fig. 15*) is 1¼-inches deep; ½-inch wide at the top. When it is necessary to join raffia strips, do it by pasting them together.

Wrap Around Waste Baskets

For the two lamp shades illustrated (*Figs. 6* and *10*) it is easy to make matching waste baskets. If the waste basket is metal, shellac it before covering it; then use a mixture of paste and glue, half-and-half, to hold the "raffia" in place. Prepare your crepe paper raffia from strips cut 1½-inches wide. Wrap them around horizontally, not perpendicularly as on the shades. It isn't necessary to paste the strips down completely; it is necessary to paste them here and there to keep them in line.

Lockstitch Waste Baskets

Select as a foundation a waste basket with straight up-and-down sides. Make a cardboard cover, without any bottom, for it. Make it a little higher than the basket, and roomy enough to allow for the "raffia" which will be wrapped around it.

Proceed as with the lamp shade, using, however, crepe paper "raffia" prepared from wider strips—strips cut 1½-inches across the grain. When the cardboard form is completely covered, slip it over the waste basket.

Multi-Color Rug

A rug of paper? Yes, and one that will wear surprisingly well. Although it cannot be tubbed, and may seem—therefore—impractical, it can be given a light coat of some such protective material as lacquer, "white" shellac, or varnish. Since new protective materials are constantly arriving on the market, it is best to consult a local paint store and to use what it recommends. Once the rug is so protected, it can be wiped off with a damp cloth.

It is not as easy to crochet a rug with paper as with yarn. The reward lies in the low cost, around two dollars, in the handsome appearance, and in the surprising wearing qualities.

Materials Needed for One:

12 folds crepe paper best quality
1 crochet hook No. 5 wooden or a large steel one.
1 Crepe Paper Twister (optional). See Chapter XII.

NOTE: *This material is sufficient to make a rug 4' by 2½'.*

Transform crepe paper into raffia-like strips according to the directions in Chapter XII. Cut the strips 2-inches wide across the grain.

Use a single crochet (sc) stitch throughout taking up both loops of each stitch. Chain 16-inches to make the backbone of the rug. Crochet around this alternating colors (in willy-nilly fashion), 1 sc in each stitch on the sides, and increasing in a fan shape at the ends to keep the work flat.

Attractive knitting bags, chair seats and pocket books can also be crocheted using the best quality crepe paper.

IT'S THE LITTLE THINGS THAT COUNT

A SPEAKING ACQUAINTANCE with three simple paper crafts will show you the way to make innumerable bright little touches for your home—touches that do for a room what costume jewelry does for a "basic black" dress. These are the sort of little items that are welcome to the maker and receiver of gifts.

The three paper crafts are Crepabraid, Wrap Around, and Build-Up Craft.

Fig. 16 (Upper left) Crepabraid carafe in three colors; Fig. 17 (Lower left) Wrap around jelly jar; Fig. 18 (Right) Build-up craft over a flower pot.

Crepabraid

This craft is illustrated by a carafe (*Fig. 16*). Made over a wine bottle that might otherwise have been thrown away, it has become a colorful re-fill bottle that will add a chirp of cheer on any side table.

See General Direction 19, *p.* 233

[214]

Materials Needed to Make One:
    1 old bottle
    1 fold crepe paper brown
    1 fold crepe paper orange
    1 fold crepe paper deep green
    Paste, glue, shellac
    A Crepe Paper Twister. (Optional) See Chapter XII.

Step 1. Shellac the entire bottle. Let it dry.

Step 2. Transform your crepe paper into "raffia" as described in Chapter XII. Cut your strips about 1-inch wide. Braid the three colors together tightly. Keep the braids as even and flat as possible.

Step 3. Beginning at the bottom, wrap the braid around bottle holding the braid down with a half-and-half mixture of paste and glue.

Step 4. Cover the cork starting at the center top.

Wrap Around Craft

The jelly jar in Figure 17 is a good example of the Wrap Around Craft. This is covered in exactly the same way as the bottle just described, except that the crepe paper raffia is not braided. Both the jar and its top are shellacked before the crepe "raffia" is applied.

The cherry design is made of Crepe Paper Twist.[19] The cherries are wound around and around and held in place with a 50-50 blend of paste and glue.

Cosmetic jars, cookie containers, vases, ink wells, and countless such items can be decorated in this way.

Build-Up Craft

An illustration of this craft is the flower pot cover shown in Figure 18.

Three collars of cardboard have been made to fit generously over the flower-pot. Each one has been wrapped around and around with crepe paper raffia. Directions for making it are in Chapter XII.

Fig. 19 "Raffia" catching two collars together.

The three collars are held together with crepe paper "raffia" threaded through a tapestry needle and run over and under the "raffia" loops as indicated by Figure 19.

See General Direction 19, *p.* 233

DÉCOUPAGE IS EVERY WOMAN'S CRAFT

INTERIOR DECORATORS WHO look down their handsome noses at many handcrafts grasp découpage to their bosoms. Popular as a decorative art in the Eighteenth Century it is acclaimed by the Twentieth Century. Smart shops catering to the wealthy have exhibits showing attic furniture decorated to the hilt with découpage (*Fig. 20*).

Fig. 20 Secretary decorated by découpage. (Photo by courtesy of Lord & Taylor.)

Furniture Decoration

Actually this craft is nothing but a method of applying to furniture, boxes, trays, etc., pictures cut from old prints and magazines.

[216]

Exhibits have featured secretaries painted black and decorated with elaborate panels of flowers and shells cut out and pasted on in beautifully contrived compositions; children's high chairs painted pink and decorated with giraffes from some old nursery books; trays with fruit, flowers and birds forming a delightful décor.

To play with this craft you need the following materials: glue, varnish, sharp scissors, and pages of designs to cut up. It isn't necessary to have the exact pictures you want. From a picture of a flower you may, for example, cut butterfly wings; from a blue sky, you may cut a bird.

First, cut out your pictures and glue them in place.

When they are dry, give the furniture a coat of "white" shellac. Allow it to dry, then rub the surface down with a piece of felt dipped in clear oil and fine powdered pumice. Brush the furniture clean, and add four to six coats of varnish giving each one, when dry, a rub-down with the oil and pumice stone.

Glossy pictures are sometimes sandpapered lightly on the back to make them adhere better.

Instead of gluing the pictures, some découpage fans prefer to varnish the wood, and after waiting for the surface to get tacky, lay the units of the design in place.

HOW TO MAKE CREPE PAPER "RAFFIA" DOLLS

THESE DOLLS, WHICH—by the way—can also be made of yarn, are all made on the same basic plan. Know it and you can make little ones for lapel gadgets, big ones for bed pillows, and middle size ones for all sorts of uses. See Susie, a lapel doll, Figure 21.

Fig. 21 Susie, a lapel doll of crepe paper.

Step-by-step directions for making a lapel doll follow, but first here is a brief description of how they're put together. The body is a long tassel, with a little stuffing at the top to form the head. The ends of the tassel are braided or tied to form two legs. The arms are one long bunch of strips tied under the head. To make the tassel, strips of crepe "raffia" are wrapped around and around a piece of cardboard. A piece of spool wire is slipped under the loops at the top of the cardboard and tied tightly. The loops at the other end are cut. There's the tassel. To tie the spool wire, simply twist the ends together tightly. When the doll is done, cut off any surplus wire.

Arms and legs can be braided or left as bunches of strips tied at the ends. Skirts are made of loops tied around the doll. The bottom loops are cut.

Susie, a Lapel Doll

To make her you need: Crepe paper, pink, white, yellow, red. One fold of each, by the way, will make a number of dolls, for only a few inches of red and yellow, for example, are needed for each.

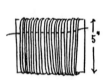   

(Left to right) Fig. 22 Step 2 in making a lapel doll; Fig. 23 Step 3 in making a lapel doll; Fig. 24 Step 4 and 5 in making a lapel doll; Fig. 25 Step 6 in making a lapel doll.

(Left to right) Fig. 26 Step 7 in making a lapel doll; Fig. 27 Step 8 in making a lapel doll; Fig. 28 Step 9 in making a lapel doll.

(Left to right) Fig. 29 Step 10 in making a lapel doll; Fig. 30 Step 11 in making a lapel doll; Fig. 31 Step 12 in making a lapel doll; Fig. 32 Step 12 in making a lapel doll

Step 1. Make crepe paper "raffia" in pink and white following the directions in Chapter XII and cutting your strips ½-inch wide. One strip of each will be more than enough.

[218]

Step 2. Wrap pink crepe "raffia" around a 5-inch piece of cardboard twelve times (*Fig. 22*).

Step 3. Slip a piece of string or better still, spool wire No. 1 under the top loops. Tie the wire tightly (*Fig. 23*).

Step 4. Cut the bottom loops. Remove the cardboard (*Fig. 24*).

Step 5. Make the head. Slip a wad of pink crepe paper, marble size, under the wire at the top loops. Under the head, tie another piece of string or wire. Tie it tightly (*Fig. 24*).

Step 6. Braid the arms with three bunches of pink crepe raffia, each containing four pieces 4-inches long. Tie wrists with spool wire or pink "raffia." The former is better (*Fig. 25*).

Step 7. Slip arms under head. Tie around waist under the arms with spool wire (*Fig. 26*).

Step 8. Braid the legs and tie the ankles with spool wire. Wrap red "raffia" shoes around the feet, and paste down the ends (*Fig. 27*).

Step 9. Make the blouse. Wrap the body with white "raffia" criss-crossing it in fichu style over the shoulders, around the neck and down in front. Paste down the ends (*Fig. 28*).

Step 10. Make the skirt. Wind red "raffia" around a piece of cardboard 1½-inches wide, twenty times. Slip spool wire under the loops at the top. Remove the cardboard. Tie the loops around the waist. Cut the bottom ends of the loops (*Fig. 29*).

Step 11. Make yellow "raffia" hair. Wrap a piece of cardboard 1½-inches wide twelve times. Paste the hair on the head. Cut the bangs. Curl the ends over a darning needle (*Fig. 30*).

Step 12. Paste on eyes and mouth—bits of blue and red paper (*Fig. 31*). Rouge the cheeks. Paste on a hair bow. Sew a safety pin to the back (*Fig. 32*).

CHAPTER XIV

How to Make Money with Paper Crafts

IT's POSSIBLE TO augment your income, or even to have full-time employment through your knowledge of and ability with paper crafts. This chapter lists many ways you can cash in by putting paper to work for you.

MAKING FLOWERS FOR RESALE

LOVELY FLOWERS OF PAPER are in demand both in and out of their natural growing season. Chapter I shows how to make eighteen popular varieties.

In many communities various groups—convents, church workers, clubs—sell the flowers which they make.

Individuals who have developed their skill to a professional point often sell their flowers.

Local shops are often customers for flowers for window displays. Bakeries, gift shops, beauty parlors, restaurants are a few of the stores that may use them regularly and are fairly sure to use them at holiday times. Easter plants in the spring, roses at all times—these are pretty sure sellers. Giant over-size flowers are also popular for window displays especially in women's clothing shops.

Teaching is another way to make money with your flower making skill. How to build up a class or classes will probably occur to you, but here are a few suggestions:

A local shopkeeper may be persuaded to let you display your personal card with a bouquet of your flowers. On the card you can advertise your classes. . . . You may be able to teach in a local club room or church parlor charging in accordance with current hourly rates. . . . Demonstrations. Perhaps you can arrange with a local dealer, who sells flower making supplies, for you to give a demonstration of flower making. From those who gather around your counter you may be able to get the nucleus of a class to be conducted in your home. . . . Lecture. When you are skilled enough you may wish to lecture before local women's clubs or other groups. Such work will help establish your reputation as a teacher. Lectures on flower making can, of course, embrace

[220]

points of interest about the flowers themselves, flower arrangement, and other allied matters. . . . A booth at a fair or a bazaar: display your flowers, sell them, and make a few for the onlookers. . . . Private lessons: shut-ins and children may be interested in taking lessons at home.

EVERYONE BUYS PARTY DECORATIONS

ENTERPRISING GIRLS AND women can develop a good little market under favorable conditions if they are recognized as expert in making party decorations. Chapters II and III give detailed instruction in the art of making favors, centerpieces and other interesting party frou-frou.

Perhaps you can sell paper nut cups, favors, and centerpieces through a local store. Bakery shops, gift shops and confectionery stores frequently carry such gaieties.

You may prefer to take special orders direct from individuals. Mothers may order centerpieces and favors for children's birthday parties. Engagements, weddings which you can learn of, if not by "word of mouth," through the local society columns of your newspaper are occasions for special favors and centerpieces; Silver and Golden Wedding Centerpieces, Stork Shower Centerpieces—all these can be sold by special order and often direct to shops.

It is well to make up some samples to show, a Santa Claus Grab Bag, a Circus Centerpiece, but offer to create favors for special occasions. This sort of thing—if a hostess is giving a farewell party to friends going to Mexico, offer to do smart little Mexican figures or baskets for her table.

Local clubs are another potential source of orders. When the holidays come around, it is pretty certain that for their dinners they will be interested in something fresh and different for favors, nut cups and centerpieces. St. Patrick's Day, Thanksgiving, Halloween, The Fourth—all offer money making possibilities to the paper crafter who is ambitious, dexterous, and imaginative.

COSTUMES CAN MAKE MONEY

ALTHOUGH THIS BRANCH of paper craft work seems less rich in money making possibilities, it is not devoid of them. Chapter V shows step-by-step instructions for making many interesting creations. When costumes must be made for a local institution's pageant you might get the order, or you might instruct groups of teachers in making them, or direct the work yourself. . . . Children love to "dress up." The child with curls loves a wig of long braids. Paper hats are something children love. Such items can be sold to gift buying aunts and grandparents. Paper leis are usually salable for dancing parties, picnics, and other gala occasions.

[221]

DECORATING FOR DANCES

DECORATING HALLS FOR dances and other big functions is a field that men seem to dominate, but it has not been deserted by women. One imaginative and energetic young woman who has made it her work has found hotels and clubs particularly regular customers. (Interesting and novel methods and techniques are clearly shown in Chapter VII.) Her services have not been confined to the city in which she lives but have been used by hotels within a two hundred mile radius of her own home. When accounts of the dances have appeared in local papers her decorations have received publicity which has spread her reputation.

It must not be overlooked that some states have laws forbidding the use of any but fireproof materials for the decoration of public places.

PAPER HANDCRAFT MAKES MONEY

THERE ARE UNLIMITED possibilities for making money by creating the novelties shown in Chapters XI, XII and XIII. Many people have made money by teaching in hospitals, settlement houses and summer camps. Some of this work is done, of course, by volunteers but there are many paid workers, too. Sometimes it is possible to organize special groups: grade teachers are often avid for new craft ideas and when acquiring them can be combined with a social evening, they will frequently form a class. Teen age youngsters are good group prospects.

In addition to teaching there are other ways of making money with paper handcrafts. Many of the items illustrated in this book can be sold direct to shops; others can be sold through direct orders from individuals.

ARTFUL GIFT WRAPPING PAYS OFF

THE WOMAN OR GIRL who is really skillful in making pretty bows in the professional way described in Chapter IV has several possibilities open to her. She may get a position in a store offering a gift wrapping service. She may be able to help establish a gift wrapping service in a community without one. If she has good taste and is reasonably fast as well as skillful, she may be able to sell her services to various merchants or proprietors of different types of establishments who are in need of special packaging jobs. One girl who is expert in this work wraps special gift packages for establishments running from a staid residential hotel that yearly presents its tenants with a Christmas Plum Pudding to a night club that is continuously presenting its feminine guests with gifts ranging from nylon hose to bottles of perfume.

With a little imagination, practically every section of this book can contribute something toward making unusual packages. For example: Favors can be used to dress up the top of a gift-wrapped parcel.

CHAPTER XV

General Directions for Using

Crepe Paper

THE DIRECTIONS WHICH are essential in making flowers are numbered 1 to 15. The others are related, chiefly, to making Party Favors, Table Decorations, Fancy Dress Costumes, Trimming Halls, Homes, Booths and other Paper Handcrafts.

Crepe paper is unique because it has a grain. This grain (note the little crinkles running across the width of the paper) gives it a touch of magic. Because of it, you can make flowers with petals and leaves that are curved, cupped, and curled like Nature's own. Because of it, you can stretch and twist crepe paper into a raffia-like material that has a hundred-and-one uses in the field of handcrafts. Because of it, you can cut it into curly and straight fringe, you can twist it into corkscrew spirals—you can manipulate it to serve in scores of different ways to decorate halls, booths, costumes, etc.

There are two kinds of crepe paper: single and Duplex. Duplex is made of two layers of single, sometimes each layer a different color. It's a big help in making some flowers, but if you can't get it, you can always make your own by pasting two layers of single together. The various articles in this book calling for "crepe paper," are to be made of single crepe, unless the directions specifically require Duplex. Only a few do.

GENERAL DIRECTION # 1

How to Cut a Strip of Crepe Paper

Slip the crepe paper from its packet the required width and cut across the paper through all layers (*Fig. 1*). You'll need fairly heavy sharp shears and a little muscle.

To make sure that your strip is an even width, use the edge of the packet as a guide.

Never forget: When directions say "cut a strip of crepe paper" you cut it across the grain as just described.

GENERAL DIRECTION # 2

How to Cut Straight Fringe

Cut a strip across the grain. Open it up. If you want to make fine

[223]

fringe, stretch the strip as much as it will stretch. If you want to make coarse fringe, stretch it just a little. Fold and refold the strip to not more than eight layers. Slash along one edge of the paper stopping as a rule in flower making about $\frac{1}{4}$ to $\frac{1}{2}$-inch short of the opposite edge (*Fig. 2*). When you've done that you've cut your paper with the grain, and you've got straight fringe which is used a lot for flower centers.

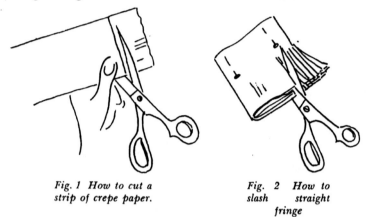

Fig. 1 *How to cut a strip of crepe paper.*   Fig. 2 *How to slash straight fringe*

GENERAL DIRECTION # 3

How to Flute Petals

These directions apply to other edges as well as petals. Hold the top of the petal (*Fig. 3*). Bring the right hand toward you, stretching the crepe over your left thumb. Make the next flute in the same way, taking care not to crush the first one. A fluted or slightly ruffled edge looks rather like a fluted pie crust.

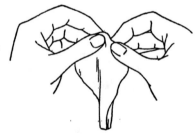

Fig. 3 *How to flute a petal.*

GENERAL DIRECTION # 4

How to Cup a Petal

Hold the petal (*Fig. 4*). Then slowly, evenly, stretch its width, pushing it out into shape. Cupping a petal gives it a cup-like curve. Many flowers have petals with such curves. The rose is one. The step-by-step directions under "Roses" in Chapter I tell you where to place the cupping, high on the petal, in its center, or at its base. They also tell you whether to cup the petals deeply or just slightly.

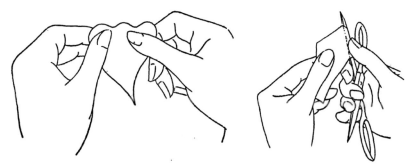

Fig. 4 (Left) How to cup a petal; Fig. 5 (Right) How to curl a petal with scissors.

GENERAL DIRECTION # 5

How to Curl a Petal

With scissors. With the petal held as illustrated (*Fig. 5*), your thumb holding the crepe over the scissors blade, draw the blade up to the edge of the petal. This is a stroking gesture that you can repeat until the petal is curled a little or a lot.

Fig. 6 How to curl a petal with a knitting needle.

With a knitting needle (*Fig. 6*). Slant your needle on the edge of the petal. Roll the petal over it to just beyond the petal's center tip. Pull your needle out.

To crush and curl a petal. Proceed as in the preceding direction. Don't pull the needle out. Crush the roll of crepe paper by pushing it from each end to the center (*Fig. 7*).

[225]

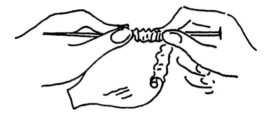

Fig. 7 How to crush and curl a petal.

GENERAL DIRECTION # 6

How to Tie Petals Together with Spool Wire

This is the way to use spool wire in tying other things, too.

With one wire. Cut off the amount of wire needed. It's usually about 8-inches, but the directions for making each flower tell exactly how much. Fold the wire in two (*Fig. 8*). Place the flower in the hairpin curve. Twist the wires together as tightly and as close to the flower as possible. Cut off the surplus crepe at the base either straight or in points. Bring the wire ends down on opposite sides of the flower's base, and twist them together underneath it (*Fig. 9*).

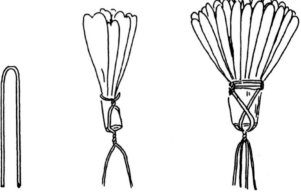

(Left to right) Fig. 8 How to tie petals with spool wire; Fig. 9 How to tie petals with one spool wire; Fig. 10 How to tie petals with two spool wires.

With two wires. Tie the second one right over the first; bring the two ends down on opposite sides from the first two. Twist all together under the flower (*Fig. 10*). Two wires are used like that sometimes on flowers that have especially large, heavy heads.

GENERAL DIRECTION # 7

How to Wrap Stems or Wires

Cut a strip [1] of crepe paper the width stated in the step-by-step directions. It's often ½-inch. Brush the base of the flower lightly with paste. Wrap one end of the strip around the base twice, stretching the strip diagonally down toward the stem. Holding the stem and strip in the position sketched (*Fig. 11*), turn the stem with the right hand at the same time stretching and guiding the strip with the left one. Wrap the entire stem diagonally downward. At the end, paste the strip down and cut off the surplus.

When a doubled strip is called for, cut the strip, then fold it along the center length—that is, across the grain. Double strips are used sometimes to make the stems thicker quickly.

Note of cheer: this wrapping business consists actually, as you'll discover, in twirling the stem as you wrap it. It's done in a jiffy.

To wrap any article around and around with crepe paper, cut a strip.[1] Open it up and stretch it around and around the article, pasting it down at the start and end and—if necessary—here and there besides.

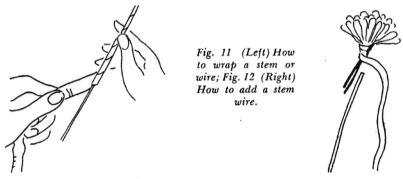

Fig. 11 (Left) How
to wrap a stem or
wire; Fig. 12 (Right)
How to add a stem
wire.

GENERAL DIRECTION # 8

How to Add Stem Wires

Place the stem wire beside the spool wire hanging from the flower base and simply wrap [7] the two together (*Fig. 12*). Let them overlap 1-inch at least. If a stem wire has to be reinforced, either for length or for strength, wrap in the additional wire in the same way.

GENERAL DIRECTION # 9

How to Add Leaves to Stem

Wrap your stem in the usual way up to the point where you want

See General Direction 1, *p.* 223; 7, *p.* 227

to insert the leaf. If the leaf has a wire stem, hold the stem against the flower's stem, and wrap the two together (*Fig. 13*). If the leaf doesn't have a wire stem, gather its base together with your fingers. Hold it close to the stem at the point where you want to insert it, and proceed with your wrapping. Be sure to wrap in at least half an inch of the leaf.

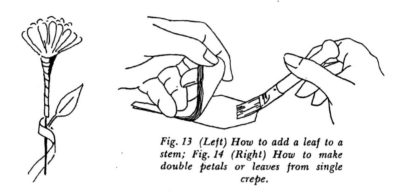

Fig. 13 (Left) How to add a leaf to a stem; Fig. 14 (Right) How to make double petals or leaves from single crepe.

GENERAL DIRECTION # 10

How to Paste Two Layers of Crepe Together

Use paste, not glue, mucilage or rubber cement. Use it sparingly, brushing it on one of the pieces of crépe with, not against, the grain. The smoother, shinier side of the crepe is the "wrong" side. The paste must be of a dry consistency. Wet, runny paste, or too much of it, will stretch, discolor—in short, ruin the crepe.

To make double petals or leaves from single crepe, place a pile of cut-out petals in front of you on your work table. Paste the top edge of the bottom petal, pressing the next petal down on top and continue until all are pasted in groups of two (*Fig. 14*). Remember that the rougher side of the crepe is the right side. The paste must be of a dry consistency and used sparingly.

To make double petals or leaves in a strip from single crepe, it is best to paste the strips together before cutting the petals. This process is used in making the African daisy and apple blossom, for example, when double petals are desired and double or Duplex crepe paper cannot be had. Proceed by cutting the strips [1] a little wider than the length of the petal. Lay one of the strips on your work table and brush paste, which is of a dry consistency, very lightly along one edge making a pasted border about 1/4-inch deep. Apply the paste with grain not against

See General Direction 1, *p.* 223

[228]

it. Paste about 6-inches, then place the second strip over the first and press the edges together. Continue until the entire strip is pasted. In cutting your strip of petals [13] be sure that the top of the pattern lies over the pasted edge.

GENERAL DIRECTION # 11

How to Paste Wire "Veins" to Leaves or Petals

Apply the paste to the wire. Press it in place with your fingers holding it down until it has adhered (*Fig. 15*). Flower wires are cotton covered. They will stick to the crepe paper when brushed with paste, but they will not adhere as well as crepe paper wrapped wires. It's really better therefore, though not necessary, to go to the extra trouble of wrapping [7] the wire "veins." Sometimes, of course, you have to do it for a color scheme. A green wire vein on a red tulip would hardly be the thing.

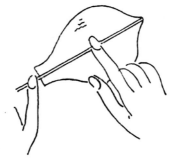

Fig. 15 How to paste a wire "vein" to a leaf or petal.

GENERAL DIRECTION # 12

How to Make Your Patterns

Trace the outlines (given in this book) of the various flower parts onto tissue paper. Paste the tissue onto wrapping paper or lightweight cardboard, then cut around the outline. On each, pencil in the three parallel lines shown on the flower pattern outlines. They indicate the grain of the crepe, a most important matter. It is helpful to write on each the name of the pattern in case you want to use it later.

GENERAL DIRECTION # 13

How to Use Your Patterns

Cut several petals or leaves at once. This is the way to do it. Cut a

See General Direction 13, *p.* 229; 7, *p.* 227

strip[1] of crepe paper ½-inch wider than the pattern you are going to use. Unfold the strip, then refold it, making sections slightly wider than the pattern. Fold it to not more than eight thicknesses of single crepe, or four of Duplex. Pin or hold the pattern in place. Cut around the pattern (*Fig. 16*). Unless otherwise stated, the grain of the crepe always runs from the tip to the base of the flower. When you put your pattern on your folded strip the three parallel lines must run in the same direction as the grain.

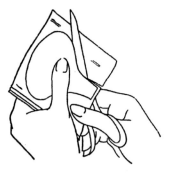

Fig. 16 How to use your patterns. Cut around the patterns.

In cutting two shades of crepe paper to make double leaves or double petals, cut a strip[1] of each color, place one strip on the other and fold the strips to not more than eight thicknesses and in such a way that when the petals are cut the colors will alternate. Then proceed to cut around your pattern as described above.

To cut a strip of petals or leaves with a pattern, fold a strip of crepe paper as described in the preceding paragraph. Lay the pattern next to the fold and cut the petals leaving the lower part of the strip in one piece (*Fig. 17*).

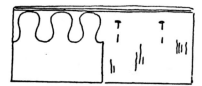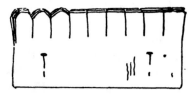

Fig. 17 (Left) Cutting a strip of petals with a pattern. (Right) Cutting petals without a pattern.

To cut a strip of petals without a pattern, cut a strip[1] of paper a little wider than the length required for the petal. Open up the strip. Refold it to not more than eight thicknesses. In refolding the paper

---

See General Direction 1, *p. 223*

measure it to make sure that it will cut a full number of petals of equal width. Sometimes no harm is done if a few petals at the end are a trifle wider or narrower than the others. To hold the eight layers together while you cut them, pin them together. A few pins are enough. Make straight cuts, with the grain, the required width and length of the petals. Don't forget to cut down the folded ends, too. Leave about ½-inch along the opposite edge uncut so that when the folded paper is opened the petals will be in one strip. Before unfolding the strip, round off or point the petal divisions *(Fig. 17)*.

When very fine petal-like divisions are required, it is much easier to cut them without a pattern.

These directions apply to petal-like and pointed fringe, too.

GENERAL DIRECTION # 14

How to Tint Flowers

It isn't necessary to tint flowers except for the dogwood petal which must be tinted. Directions in Chapter I tell how. It's fun though to tint some of them, for a little shading here and there may make them more natural looking. Pink roses are often improved with a blush of rouge added to a few petal tips. Orange zinnias look handsome when their petal ends are tipped with a deeper tone. Observe natural flowers and, if you wish, tint your own to copy them.

You can use pastel crayons, dry pigment powder, rouge and burnt cork. Apply the color with a bit of cotton. Rub it in lightly along the grain of the crepe blending it in at the edges.

GENERAL DIRECTION # 15

How to Gather Crepe Paper

Cut a strip,[1] then gather it across the grain by hand or by machine.

Ruffles can sometimes be made this simple way that avoids sewing; cut your strip of crepe. Crease it across the grain down the center. Place a ruler, pencil, or knitting needle in the crease. Push the crepe together from both ends *(Fig. 18)*. Remove the inserted article. Such ruffles are

Fig. 18 Pushing the crepe together from both ends.

See General Direction 1, *p.* 223

often tied in place, a piece of string or wire being inserted before the ruler is pulled out.

Sometimes you can simply paste or tie the paper in gathers.

GENERAL DIRECTION # 16

How to Make Crushed Crepe Paper

Cut off the approximate amount needed. Stretch it completely. Place the paper on a flat surface pinching (*Fig. 19*) small portions of it with your finger tips. Continue until the entire surface is crushed. Smooth it out slightly. Brush the surface to be covered with paste, lay the paper over it and press it down. Sometimes crushed paper is sewed in place. In spite of its rather sad name, crushed crepe is a joy. It can be used for all sorts of coverings, from stage fireplaces, tree trunks and wigs to bases for table centerpieces, box coverings, doll furniture.

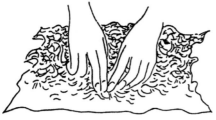

Fig. 19 How to make
crushed crepe paper.

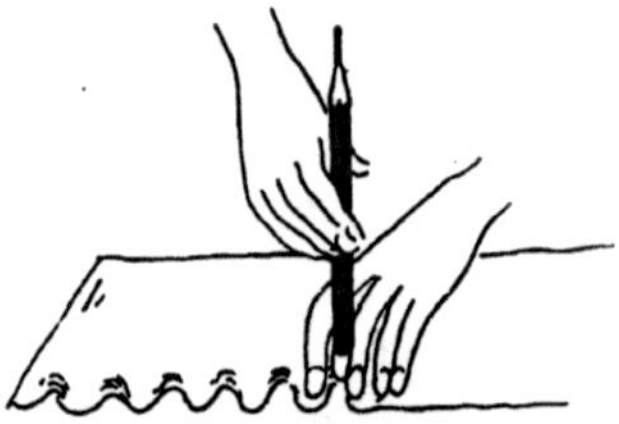

Fig. 20   How to
make finger scal-
lops.

GENERAL DIRECTION # 17

How to Make Finger Scallops

Cut a strip [1] of crepe paper the desired width. Place your left hand on one edge of it with your fingers in the position shown. With the index finger of your right hand, or with the eraser end of a pencil, push the edge of the paper down between your two fingers (*Fig. 20*). Move your fingers along the strip repeating the process.

These finger scallops are a pretty edging for crepe paper costumes and many party favors.

GENERAL DIRECTION # 18

How to Make Twisted Petals

Through the entire fold, cut strips of paper [1] the width you have decided upon. Shake out a strip and refold it until you have eight layers.

See General Direction 1, *p.* 223

Stretch them slightly. At this point it's a help to pin your layers together here and there. Along one edge slash the paper at even intervals and to the same depth. An inch apart is a good general width. Take your scissors and round off the corners of the petal divisions. Unpin, open up your strip, and start twisting. This is the way to do it. Holding the edge of a petal division as shown in the sketch (*Fig. 21*), with one hand twist the petal away from you, with the other twist it toward you. Be firm about this and make a complete twist. A pretty variation can be secured by cutting out ovals of crepe, about the size of the petal ends, in a contrasting color and placing them on the petal ends as you do your twisting. Twisted petals make an effective trim for many items (*Fig. 22*).

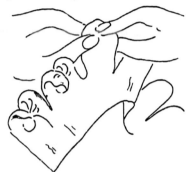 

Fig. 21 *How to make twisted petals.*   Fig. 22 *Twisted petals completed.*

GENERAL DIRECTION # 19

How to Make Crepe Paper Twist

Cut a strip [1] across the grain. Open it up. Twist one end to a point, then with your fingers in the position sketched (*Fig. 23*), stretch the paper with the fingers of your left hand as you roll it to a twist between the thumb and forefinger of your right hand. A very fine twist can be made by cutting the strip $\frac{1}{4}$ to $\frac{1}{2}$-inch wide.

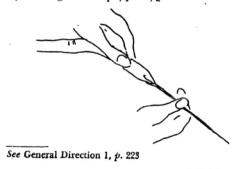

Fig. 23 *How to make crepe paper twist.*

See General Direction 1, *p. 223*

GENERAL DIRECTION # 20

How to Cut Fringe

Straight fringe is cut with the grain of the crepe as described in General Direction #2. It can, of course, be cut different lengths, different widths and to varying fineness.

Curly fringe is cut across the grain of the crepe. The paper automatically curls when so cut. Curly fringe is widely used for room decorations, for festooning around ceiling lights, for draping over walls and booths.

To make wide widths of curly fringe, unfold your crepe paper and cut off pieces of the desired length. Fold the lower end up to within an inch or two of the top. Redouble the paper two or three times, put a few pins in here and there to hold it together then, beginning at either the right or left side, cut the fringe as fine or as coarse as you wish cutting through all layers at once (*Fig. 24*). Leave the heading of "an inch or two" at the top uncut, of course. Unfold the paper and stretch the fringe slightly. To tack this in place, fold the uncut edge over once or twice to give a firm heading. Tacks or pins, Scotch tape or paste can be used to hold it in place.

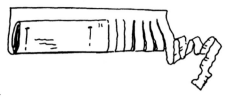

Fig. 24 How to cut curly fringe.

GENERAL DIRECTION # 21

How to Join Two Widths of Crepe Paper

Crepe is only 20-inches wide. It is, therefore, necessary sometimes to piece it. This can be done in either one of these three ways that seems easiest to you. Overlap the two pieces to be joined about 1/2 inch and join them by stitching them together on the machine, by pasting them, or pressing Scotch tape down over the joining. Stitching is firmest.

In some cases crepe paper can also be seamed on the machine just as cloth is. In other words, place the two pieces with the right (that's the dull) sides together. Stitch the two together about 1/2-inch from the edge. Press the seam open—using your fingers, not an iron.

GENERAL DIRECTION # 22

Fish Net Drapery

This can be used—among other things—for a wall decoration or for a table covering. It requires strong, sharp shears. Remove the fold of crepe paper from its package, and pin all the layers together, using about four long pins. Along one folded edge cut slits evenly spaced, say 1-inch apart, stopping 1-inch short of the other edge. When all the slits are cut along one side, repeat the slitting process on the other side and in exactly the same way, cutting between the slits just made (*Fig. 25*). Take out the pins, unfold the paper, and there's your net.

Fig. 25 How to cut fish net drapery.

GENERAL DIRECTION # 23

How to Make Pompons

To make a pompon of fringed crepe paper, cut a strip[1] of crepe paper the desired width. Open up the strip, and refold it to about eight thicknesses. Put a few pins through the eight layers to hold them together while you cut each edge to within $\frac{1}{2}$-inch of the center into fringe. If you want fine fringe, stretch the paper before cutting it. Remove the pins and shake out the strip. Gather it with your hands through the center and tie it tightly with spool wire (*Fig. 26*). To tie

Fig. 26 (Left) How to make pompons of fringed crepe paper.

Fig. 27 (Right) Pompon of crepe paper ruffles.

with the wire, bend it to hairpin shape. Place the fringed strip in the curve, and twist the wire ends together tightly under the strip. Push the fringed ends together to form a ball. If it isn't round and fat enough, make another, or two or three more and join them all by twisting their tie-wires together.

See General Direction 1, *p.* 223

To make a pompon of crepe paper ruffles, proceed in the same way using a strip of paper fluted [8] on each edge instead of fringed (*Fig. 27*).

(Left to right) Fig. 28 Tassel made with a strip of crepe paper cut across the grain. Fig. 29 Tassel made with fringe cut across the grain of the crepe; Fig. 30 Making tassel sketched in Figure 29.

GENERAL DIRECTION # 24

How to Make Crepe Paper Tassels

They may be made of crepe paper cut into fringe across the grain (*Fig. 29*) or with the grain (*Fig. 28*).

For an 8-inch tassel like Figure 28, cut a strip [1] of crepe paper across the grain 8-inches wide and 20-inches long. For quick and easy cutting fold the strip to four or eight thicknesses. Pin the layers together with a few pins. Slash one edge into 1/4-inch wide fringe to within 1-inch of the opposite edge. Shake the strip out and refold it to two layers. Brush the end of a ribbon, cord, or length of crepe paper rope with paste and place it at one end of the fringe, on the uncut edge. Roll the strip around the pasted end. Fasten the end of the strip with paste. For the head of the tassel, cut a piece of paper, silver, gold, or any attractive color, and paste it in place.

For a tassel like Figure 29, make curly fringe,[20] i.e., fringe cut across the grain of the crepe. Tie a big knot in the end of the cord, ribbon or rope, and with the knotted end upright tie the fringed strip (the uncut edge) around it (*Fig. 30*). Take hold of the rope and reverse the position of the fringe. One inch below the rope, tie the tassel tightly to form the head. It can be tied with spool wire [6] or with a bit of yarn or ribbon. Ribbon ends can be pasted rather than tied.

Tassels are useful for room decorations to hang from lights, on pillars, from balconies, or to accent swagged draperies. They are decorative for booths at fairs, bazaars, and for party caps, and favors.

See General Direction 3, *p.* 224; 1, *p.* 223; 20, *p.* 234; 6, *p.* 226

GENERAL DIRECTION # 25

How to Make Evergreen Garlands

Across the entire fold of crepe paper, cut strips 8 to 10-inches in width.[1] Open up a strip and refold it to no more than eight thicknesses. Stick some pins through all the layers to hold them together while you cut along each edge. Cut 3-inches deep at 2½-inch intervals, and cut the divisions to points; cut the opposite side in the same way, but slash your crepe so that the points will not be exactly opposite the points on the other edge. Open the strip up, gather it with needle and thread through the center on the machine or by hand (*Fig. 31*). Cup each pointed division slightly at the base. Fasten one end of the garland in place, then holding the other end, twirl it around and around until it is fat and fluffy. Narrower garlands are useful, too. In making a 5-inch wide garland, cut the slits 1¾-inches wide at 1-inch intervals.

Fig. 31 How to make evergreen garlands.

GENERAL DIRECTION # 26

How to Make Quick Fake Roses

How wide do you wish to make your rose? Six inches, say? Then cut a strip of crepe paper about 6-inches wide.[1] Fold it in two down the center length, but do not crease the fold. Fold one end of the strip down

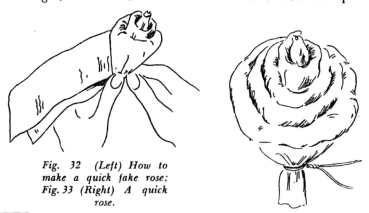

Fig. 32 (Left) How to make a quick fake rose; Fig. 33 (Right) A quick rose.

See General Direction 1, *p.* 223

diagonally and wind the rest of the strip around this *(Fig. 32)* gathering the strip slightly at the bottom until your rose is about 6-inches across. Fasten the end down with paste and tie the base securely with spool wire [6] *(Fig. 33)*.

Fig. 34 (Left) How to make panelled fringe; Fig. 35 (Right) Panelled fringe.

GENERAL DIRECTION # 27

How to Make Panelled Fringe

This trick with crepe paper will give you a stretch of panelled fringe 10 feet long and 20-inches wide. You can, of course, increase its length and width by pinning a matching job to it, and you can cut it to almost any length you wish. Take your fold of crepe paper from its packet and without unfolding it pin the layers together with several long pins. Along one 20-inch side, cut the paper every half inch to within 2-inches of the other side *(Fig. 34)*. Open it up, and there's the panelled fringe *(Fig. 35)*. This is popular for draping around ceiling lights, over balconies and for other points of interest in a dance hall.

GENERAL DIRECTION # 28

How to Make Crepe Paper Rope

This sleight-of-hand is enough fun to be a game. For a ¼-inch wide rope, cut the paper into a strip 5-inches wide.[1] For rope 1½-inches thick, use the whole width of the crepe paper.

The general idea is to stretch the crepe paper strip as far as it will stretch, and then twist it, and twist it, and twist it. Fold it in the middle and the twisted sections will spiral around each other in rope fashion.

The easiest way to do it is for two people to work together. Each one stretches the paper, then each starts twisting his end. To do a thorough job on this twisting, tie a loop in the end of the strip, put a pencil through it, and twirl the pencil around and around, and around some more. When the time has come to fold the twisted strip in two, take care not to let the strip untwist. Simply lay the two halves together. They'll do the rest. If the paper hasn't been twisted tightly enough there won't

See General Direction 6, *p.* 226; 1, *p.* 223

be much spring to it. The two strands can, of course, be aided by more twisting.

GENERAL DIRECTION # 29

How to Make Crepe Paper Streamers

Cut crepe paper into strips [1] across the grain. That's all there is to it! Streamers are usually about 3-inches wide. They can also be purchased ready-made.

GENERAL DIRECTION # 30

How to Use Paste with Crepe Paper

In pasting crepe paper to plain paper a few words of warning are indicated. Paste must be used sparingly, and must be of dry consistency. When crepe paper is being pasted to non-crepe or plain paper, put the paste on the plain paper, lay the crepe over it, and press it, if necessary, along the grain of the crepe.

GENERAL DIRECTION # 31

How to Make Crushed Crepe Paper Tubes

These can be made over any smooth cylinder. A pencil or knitting needle can be used for small ones, a flag or dowel stick, about ¼-inch in diameter for medium size ones, and a broom stick for large ones.

Cut off enough crepe paper to wrap several times around the cylinder (*Fig. 36*). The grain of the crepe must run from top to bottom. After wrapping the paper, paste down the end lightly. Place the end of the cylinder against a table and push the crepe paper down hard. Begin toward the bottom of the cylinder (*Fig. 37*) and push down a small sec-

Fig. 36 (Left) Starting to make a crushed crepe paper tube. Fig. 37 (Right) Crushing a crepe paper tube.

See General Direction 1, *p.* 223

tion at a time. After the entire tube is pushed down, remove it from the cylinder, and stretch it out slightly.

GENERAL DIRECTION # 32

How to Make Crepe Paper Beading

Cut two strips [1] of crepe paper, each a different color, about ½-inch wide. Put one strip on top of the other, then with your fingers holding the double strip firmly as shown (*Fig. 38*), twist it tightly by turning your right hand away from you, your left toward you. Move your fingers along the strip placing your right fingers in the spot where your left ones have just been and giving a good firm twist each time. This will give you a beading of alternate colors (*Fig. 39*) which can be pasted to costumes, favors, lamp shades and many other items as a decorative trim.

Beading can be made much narrower and slightly wider; ½-inch, a stingy half, is a good average width.

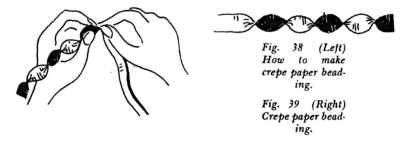

Fig. 38 (Left) How to make crepe paper beading.

Fig. 39 (Right) Crepe paper beading.

GENERAL DIRECTION # 33

How to Drape Crepe Paper

Two can do this easier than one. Open a fold of crepe paper. Cut off a little less than you need. With one person holding each end, stretch the paper slowly but not tenderly. Crepe paper is strong. When all the stretch is pulled from it, it is ready to drape. Soft, yet crisp, it will, when draped, lie in graceful folds which will retain their sculptured look.

GENERAL DIRECTION # 34

How to Cover a Wall Panel with Crepe Paper

Crepe paper provides color inexpensively. It can be used to cover a wall surface, as in a store window or in a hall, where fresh but not permanent color is wanted. As it comes in a 20-inch width it is hung in 20-inch panels. To hang it smoothly, fold over one end several times to make a sturdy heading. Tack that heading in place at the top of the wall

See General Direction 1, *p.* 223

[240]

surface to be covered. Cut the bottom of the crepe paper several inches short of the floor. For a 6-foot high wall, cut it about 8-inches from the floor. Fold the bottom edge over several times, just as you did the top. Now stretch the paper down slowly and evenly and tack the folded bottom edge in place. To stretch the paper evenly use this device: Wrap the paper at the bottom around a yard stick several times. Pull the yardstick down.

WIRE CHART

THROUGHOUT THIS BOOK wires are called for. They are especially important in making flowers and party favors. The wires needed are sold in shops as "flowers makers' " or "artificial flower" wires. They are cotton covered and come in green, and—in some weights—in white.

Numbers are used, in this book, to specify the weight wire needed for specific purposes. Unfortunately, the weights of wires are not like thread, for example, standardized with numbers. The numbers used in the chart below and throughout the book were chosen because they are used by one of the large distributors of flower wires and in many instruction books. Underneath each number in the chart is a black line of the width of the wire in question. If your local merchants are not familiar with the numbers, 1, 10, 15, etc. the line may help them locate the right wire for you.

Throughout the book where "Materials Required" are listed, the quantity of wires has been estimated with the lengths given below. If "3 No. 15" wires are called for, three 36-inch length wires are needed.

TYPE OF WIRE	LENGTH	SOME USES	COLOR	NOTE
No. 1, Spool	10 yards	This is for tying. It is sometimes called "tie-wire." It is used, among other things, for tying petals together in flower making.	White	The wire sometimes used around milk bottle tops can be used to replace spool wire, but it is harder to use and is less satisfactory. Spool wire is easily cut with scissors.

No. 2 Spool (Exactly like No. 1, except in color. It's green.)

Medium Weight

No. 9.	36-inches	Used for veins of leaves, stems of small flowers and for party favors where a very pliable wire is needed.	Green	Easy to cut with scissors.

Medium Weight

No. 10   (Exactly like No. 9, except that it is white.)

Medium Heavy
Weight
No. 7   36-inches   For stems for bigger   Green   Should be cut with
and/or/stiff stemmed   wire pliers or cutters.
flowers; for bodies of
wire dolls and for con-
struction of center-
pieces.

Heavy Weight
No. 15   36-inches   For stems of big and/   Green   Must be cut with pli-
or/very stiff stemmed   ers or wire cutters.
flowers; for branches.
For construction of
centerpieces and big
wire dolls.

$\mathcal{I}ndex$

Index

Printed in the United States
92642LV00002B/163/A

9 781432 608392